Learning Design with Alias® StudioTools™

A Hands-on Guide to Modeling and Visualization in 3D

⊙Alias | LearningTools

ACKNOWLEDGEMENTS

Cover & book design:
Ian McFadyen

Cover Image:
Fridolin Beisert

Production designer:
Mike Barker

Editorial services:
Erica Fyvie

Technical editor:
Diego Pacitto

DVD Production:
Roark Andrade, Julio Lopez

Jr. Project Manager:
Skye Bjarnason

Project Manager:
Carla Sharkey

Product Manager, Learning Tools and Training:
Danielle Lamothe

Director, Learning Tools and Training:
Michael Stamler

LEARNING DESIGN WITH ALIAS® STUDIOTOOLS™

Alias®
StudioTools™ > Techniques

Discover industry-tested solutions & insider tips for creating effective packaging designs & consumer products.

These DVDs explore the workflows and techniques recommended for creating effective packaging design and creating sound consumer products with Alias StudioTools.

If you want to become a pro, what better way than to learn from one! You will benefit from instructor Lee Irvine's years of design experience and his in-depth knowledge of the tools and techniques made possible with Alias StudioTools.

For more information visit
www.alias.com/learningtools

◉Alias | LearningTools

⊘Alias | design solutions

Advantage
> by Design

THE DESIGN BUSINESS is no place for the timid. In fact, bold, eye-catching design can be the difference between a breakthrough product and one that blends into a pale beige landscape. Alias Design Solutions deliver a competitive advantage by allowing designers to create innovative, head-turning products that demand attention.

The latest release of Alias design software products – **Alias StudioTools**™13, **Alias ImageStudio**™3 and **Alias PortfolioWall**®3 – allow designers to create, craft, collaborate, and convey their designs in one complete flow – concentrating on ideas, not tools. When designers are focused on what they do best, their products will have an advantage, by design.

For more information on Alias Design Solutions including our complete range of consulting, training, and custom engineering services, visit **www.alias.com/design**.

⊘Alias®
imagination's **engine**™

Alias
DesignStudio® **&** Alias
ImageStudio™
Free 90-day trial software included on DVD

ABOUT THE AUTHOR: Fridolin T. Beisert

Fridolin T. Beisert was born in Hamburg, Germany, where he grew up inspired by his two loving parents, a doctor and a children's book illustrator, as well as his older brother, a film director.

In researching the best school for his own ambition and talent, Fridolin eventually went to the U.S. to pursue a degree from the Art Center College of Design in Los Angeles, entering as an industrial design student. It was during this time as a student when he started to discover his passion for the design process and creative problem solving. He was awarded scholarships from both Art Center and Alias and also received the prestigious Universal Studios internship, which enabled him to explore his interest in entertainment design. Subsequently, Fridolin received his Bachelor of Science in both Product and Entertainment Design and was recognized with the additional title of "Distinction," Art Center's highest graduating honor. Samples of Fridolin's work are included in the Alias StudioTools Gallery.

Directly after graduation he was hired to work for Sony® Playstation® in Tokyo to design video game titles. It was Japan's rich cultural history fused with its technological advancements that fascinated Fridolin's inspiration and still influences his personal artwork to this day.

During his stay in Asia, he formed his own creative concept design consultancy, Red Thread. His clients include Designworks, Ford Motor Company, Lincoln/Mercury, Mattel, Markenfilm, Stuart Karten Design, MJZ, HSI/Venus Entertainment, H.R. Giger, Gensler, Young & Rubicam, Landor, Grey Advertising, Dunhill, Alias, Earthlink, Heineken, Phillips, Sony, and Biodesign. His work has been published in Graphis, Business Week, Axis, Interni, Stern, and has been shown on The Discovery Channel and in a Mercedes Benz documentary.

Fridolin recently returned to his alma mater to teach both Alias StudioTools and Industrial Design as a full-time instructor, sharing his rich experience with the designers of the future. Besides his digital capabilities, he is currently expanding his horizon even further by studying traditional papermaking and printmaking, while simultaneously pursuing his own personal art and design projects.

A very special thanks from the author, Fridolin Beisert goes out to:

My parents, Heide-Helene and Michael, and my brother Florian, my girlfriend, the production team at Alias, Laura Silva, Marty Smith, Karen Hofmann, Norm Schureman, Michelle Katz, Nate Young, Michael Plesh, Paul Le Tourneur, Manuel Montes, Dallas Good,Tony Zepeda, Nijo Watanabe, Fredrik Buch, Matthias Beeguer, Richard Lassalle, Steven Montgomery, Walid Saba, Bobby Zee, Gustaf Aspegren, Julia Kopelson, my teaching assistants at Art Center and my hardworking students that contributed to this book.

A special thanks goes out to:

David Atkinson, Mariann Barsolo, Carmela Bourassa, Blair Brenot, Ken Bryson, Sylvana Chan, Chris Cheung, James Christopher, Thomas Heermann, Rachael Jackson, Martti Lemieux, Robert Lin, Lorraine McAlpine, Lenni Rodrigues, Uwe Rossbacher, Margaret Rowlands, Michael Stamler.

We would like to send out a special thanks to Fridolin Beisert's students at California's Art Center College of Design for providing the samples at the end of each chapter in this book.

FOREWORD

C. Martin Smith | Product Design Department

The design profession, as a whole, has undergone profound changes in the past ten years since the emergence of applied design in the early part of the 20th century.

Designers from all fields have struggled to keep pace with the rapid evolution of software and hardware technologies that support their creative endeavors. Workshops, online courses, and books like this one have emerged to fill this knowledge gap and help designers communicate more effectively with their creativity.

Several significant factors set this book apart from other efforts. First and foremost, it begins with the author. Mr. Beisert is a designer and, as such, approaches the learning and utilization of Alias software from that point of view. It's not so much about the buttons, menus and so on (although that is certainly part of it); it's about which functions to use in the creative pursuit of product and surface development. His approach is unique: integrating the software into the workflow of design projects.

His method is a successful one, proven time and time again in the classrooms and studios of Art Center College of Design, as well as from his experiences as a professional designer. He believes, and I agree, that a greater understanding of the digital 3D world, as represented by Alias software, elevates the student's 2D sketching to a more informed and sophisticated level. We have witnessed a marked improvement in mock-ups, models and other representations of form after exposure to working in the virtual world of three-dimensional space.

This book is structured with two components: Tools and Lessons. Each chapter begins with a thorough description of functions and the many ways they can be utilized. The lessons consist of exercises that will help the reader become familiar with the tools. Hence, this book is a successful union of theory and application.

Ultimately, the value of this book is how the methodologies described in each chapter enable the designer to move beyond just one or two areas of specialization. The author's goal is to empower creative individuals with a process and the means to design anything.

C. Martin Smith
Chair

Product Design Department
Art Center College of Design

Table of Contents

Introduction

Chapter01   Modeling with primitives

Chapter02   Additive design

Chapter03   Subtractive design

Chapter04   Industrial design

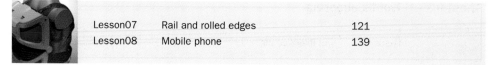

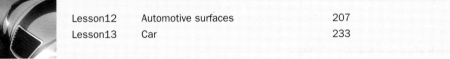

HOW TO USE THIS BOOK

This book is designed to help new users design in Alias StudioTools. *Learning Design with Alias® StudioTools™* will teach you the most efficient way to build designs quickly and effectively. As you work through the lessons in this book, you will learn the principles of industrial design through hands-on project based learning accompanied with visual illustrations to guide you through each lesson. This book will also explore workflows for adding detail to designs through modeling, animation and rendering.

Beginner – If this is your first experience with 3D software, we suggest that you glance over each lesson before you complete it. This will give you a better understanding of what is going to happen before you tackle the software directly.

Intermediate – If you are already familiar with the world of 3D, you can dive in and complete the lessons as written.

Expert – Experts can run through the lessons in this book at a quicker pace. The location of the tools and the terminology found in the software will be the most helpful aspect of this book.

Updates to this book

In an effort to ensure your continued success through the lessons in this book, please visit our Web site for the latest updates available:

www.alias.com/learningtools_updates/

Alias packaging

This book can be used with StudioTools 13, DesignStudio 13 or StudioTools Personal Learning Edition, as the lessons included here focus on functionality shared among all three software packages.

As a bonus feature, this hands-on book will also introduce you to rendering in Alias ImageStudio.

DVD-ROM

The DVD-ROM accompanying this book contains several resources to accelerate your learning experience including:

- Instructor-led overviews to guide you through the projects in the book

- Scene files

- A 90-day trial of Alias ImageStudio*

- A 90-day trial of Alias DesignStudio*

* To access your serial number, please see the start-here.html page on the DVD-ROM included with this book.

Please note that the trial versions included in this book do not include technical support. If you encounter any problems while installing the software, please visit www.alias.com/support for additonal instructions. You may also contact your local sales office or reseller for help. To find an Alias sales office or reseller, please visit www.alias.com/purchase.

Installing lesson files – before beginning the lessons in this book, you will need to install the lesson support files. Copy the project directories found in the support_files folder on the DVD disc directory onto your computer. We recommend that you install the contents of the DVD-ROM before proceeding with the *Learning Design with Alias® StudioTools™* lessons.

ROEL PUNZALAN

"Roel made a very tasteful concept for an ArtCenter Health Center. I like the inviting composition with the view over the lawn. Notice how just about every shape used is a primitive cube, but through texturing and lighting he achieved a very warm feel to the space. The left glass also has a reflection which suggests that there is more to the environment than the eye can see."

SO YON CHRISTINE PARK

"I like this image because it is very playful and uses cheerful colors. Notice the two small pillows on the couch: they are slightly irregular, suggesting that maybe someone was just in the room enjoying the warm fireplace. The high ceiling together with the stairs in the background adds a lot of depth and space, almost like a loft. Christine also placed some artwork on the walls, which makes the rendering very inviting."

Chapter One >

Modeling with primitives

This lesson will teach you step by step how to get started modeling a table and lamp using primitive geometry. You will add lights and shaders to the scene and create a rendering to see your results.

In this lesson you will learn how to:

- Set-up the window layout and the measurements;

- Create primitive shapes, transform geometry, set pivots, duplicate objects, modify CVs and delete geometry;

- Use diagnostic shading, create lights, assign shaders and direct render your scene;

- Save and restore your file;

- Create a final rendering;

- Customize your marking menu.

Setting up your project

When you launch Alias StudioTools 13 for the first time, the overall window layout will likely look as follows:

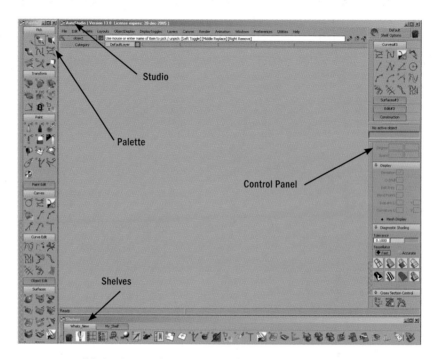

Window layout when you launch StudioTools for the first time

There are four main areas: **Studio** (with an empty workspace), **Palette**, **Shelves** and **Control Panel**. Before you start, change the layout as outlined in the following steps to maximize the workspace and maintain consistency with this tutorial.

> **Tip:** *If the Control Panel is not visible, click on* **Windows** *and select it from the pull-down menu.*

1   Changing the layout

- Close the **Shelves** window by clicking on the **X** box in its upper right-hand corner.

- Next, go to **Studio** → **Preferences** → **Interface** → **Palette/Shelves layout** → □.

  *In this tutorial, the path indicated always starts with the window where the function is located (**Studio** or **Palette** or **Control Panel**). The □ at the end indicates that there is an option window to that function that you should open.*

Tip: *To bring the Shelves window back, you can also click on **Windows**.*

Notice that the options window has four executable buttons:

Reset (resets all the options to their default).

Save (saves any changes you made, but does not execute them).

Exit (leaves the window without executing anything).

Go (this will execute the options you selected and exit the window).

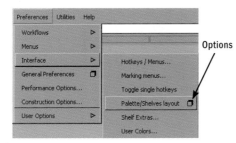

Click on the options next to the tool

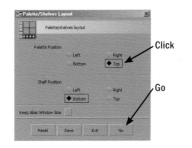

Options for the Palette/Shelves Layout window

- In the options, check the **Top** box under **Palette Position** and click on **Go**.

  This will change the layout and put the Palette window on the top.

2   Start a new file

- Go to **Studio** → **File** → **New**.

  *You should now see the three Orthographic views (**top**, **side** and **back**) and the Perspective view open (**Persp [Camera]**).*

Note: *The following lessons have been written using Alias AutoStudio 13. The lessons in this book are compatible with the complete line of StudioTools software packages. However, it is important to note that for anyone using DesignStudio or Studio, the naming convention of the default modeling windows differ from their names in AutoStudio and SurfaceStudio. If you are working in either Studio or DesignStudio, make a note that when asked to work in the side window in the following lessons, you should use the front window, and when asked to work in the back view, use the right window.*

Changing the grid

StudioTools allows you to work in different measuring units (inches, centimeters, etc.), and in different scales. Some of the presets and scales become very important once you start to use rapid prototyping or export your wire file into a different software. Depending on which package of StudioTools you are working on, the default settings may vary. In order to be consistent with this tutorial, change the presets to centimeters as follows:

1 Construction options

- Go to **Studio** → **Preferences** → **Construction Options** ...

- In the **Options**, click on **Units** and then **Linear**. In the pull-down menu that appears, set the **Units** to **cm**.

- When done, make sure to check the box **Reset Grids**.

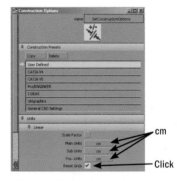

Setting the Construction Options

2 Grid spacing

Set the grid spacing to 1 unit:

- Go to **Palette** → **Construction** → **Grids Preset** → ❑.

  This will pop-up the preset grid options.

- In the window, change the **Grid Spacing** to **1**, and the **Perspective Grid Extent** to **40**.

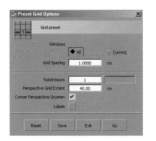

Changing the Preset Grid Options

Chapter One

- Click on **Go** for the new settings to take effect.

Try navigating the camera around by holding down **Shift** + **Alt** *(on your keyboard) and any of the three mouse buttons:*

Left Mouse Button [LMB] = tumble or rotate
(works only in Perspective view);

Middle Mouse Button [MMB] = track;

Right Mouse Button [RMB] = zoom.

3   Testing the grid

To ensure that you are working with the correct settings, bring out a primitive cube:

- Go to **Palette** → **Surfaces** → **Primitives** → **Cube**.

- Click anywhere in the top window to place the cube.

Depending on which package of StudioTools you are using, the cube will either be exactly a size 1 on the grid or exponentially larger.

- Go to **Palette** →
  Transform → **Scale**.

- Type **1** in the **Promptline** and press **Enter**.

File	Edit	Delete	Layouts	ObjectDisplay	DisplayTgls
	object		<>	Enter SCALE (ABS):1_	
	Category			DefaultLayer	

Promptline

The cube should now be exactly 1 grid unit large, regardless of the version of StudioTools that you are working on.

- Delete the cube by pressing the **Delete** key on your keyboard.

Note: Remember to first scale every primitive down to 1 for this tutorial.

Table top

After you have set-up the correct grid spacing, begin modeling by bringing out a primitive cube and scaling it into a rectangular shape.

Note: Use the right mouse button unless otherwise noted.

Lesson 01
Table top

1 Primitive cube

- Go to **Palette** → **Surfaces** → **Primitives** → **Cube**.

- In the **promptline**, enter the new cube position (**X Y Z**) using either commas or spaces between the numbers:

    | Layouts | ObjectDisplay | DisplayTgls | Layers | Canvas |
    | <> | Enter new cube position (x,y,z) (ABS) :0 0 4_ | | | |
    | | DefaultLayer | | | |

    Enter the cube position

    0 0 4

- Press **Enter** on your keyboard.

    This will place the cube 4 units above the origin (in the Z-axis).

2 Scaling the cube

Scale the cube into the rectangular table surface:

- Go to **Palette** → **Transform** → **Nonp Scale**.

- In the **promptline**, enter the new cube scale (**X Y Z**):

    6 6 0.5

- Press **Enter**.

    This will non-proportionally scale the cube into a flat rectangle.

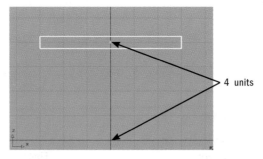

Side view of the rectangular shape

Tip: Hold down **Alt** + **Shift** and click+drag the **Middle** or **RMB** in any of the Orthographic views to get a better look at your geometry. Notice that the **MMB** tracks while the **RMB** zooms in and out.

Table legs

1 Primitive cylinder

- Go to **Palette** → **Surfaces** → **Primitives** → **Cylinder** → ❑.

  In the options, click on the number 2 next to Caps with the left mouse button, and keep it pressed until a pull-down menu appears.

- Select **0** for the caps.

  The caps are the top and bottom lids of the cylinder. Since they would not show in the rendering, it is better to leave them out in order to save memory.

  Set the cylinder caps to 0

- Click on **Go.**

- Enter the new position into the **promptline:**

      -2.5 -2.5 3.25

- Press **Enter.**

2 Setting the pivot

In order to scale the cylinder correctly, first make sure that it is a size 1:

- **Palette** → **Transform** → **Scale.**

- Type **1** into the **promptline** and press **Enter.**

Now you will set the pivot at the top of the cylinder so that it will scale down from it.

- **Palette** → **Transform** → **Local** → **Set Pivot.**

- Enter the following numbers in the **promptline:**

      -2.5 -2.5 3.75

- Press **Enter.**

  Notice that the green pivot jumps from its original centered location to the top of the cylinder.

Pivot point (green)

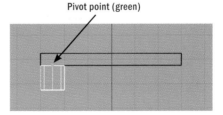

New pivot point position

Lesson 01

3 Scaling the leg

With the cylinder still selected, go to:

- Palette → Transform → Nonp Scale

- In the **promptline**, enter the new scale:

    0.5 0.5 3.75

- Press **Enter**.

This will scale the cylinder down from the new location of the leg.

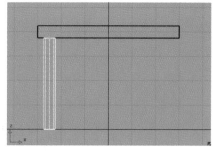

Scaled table leg

4 Duplicating

Once the leg is scaled correctly, you will duplicate it by going to:

- Studio → Edit → Duplicate → Object → ❐.

- In **Translation**, enter 5 into the **middle** column:

The three columns represent the X Y Z axes from left to right.

- Click on **Go**.

This will make a duplicate of the cylinder and move it 5 units in the Y-axis at the same time.

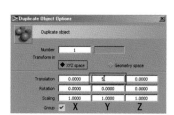

Change the translation to 5

5 Moving around

Now that you have some geometry, try to navigate in the Perspective window.

- Click on the top bar of the Perspective window to activate it.

- On your keyboard, hold down **Alt + L**.

*This will zoom into the active table leg. Alt I L is the hotkey combination for the **Look** at feature.*

- Then hold down **Alt + Shift** and use the **LMB** to tumble (rotate) around your geometry.

A viewing panel will appear in the upper left-hand corner of the Perspective view, which enables you to quickly select any of the default views or to look

at active geometry. In addition, it also has a bookmark feature with which you can save a particular view for later access.

Tip: *Remember to use the **RMB** and **MMB** together with **Alt** + **Shift** to zoom and track.*

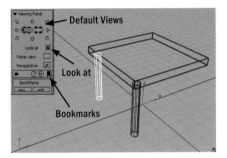

Using the viewing panel

Another very useful navigation tool is the **Point of Interest** feature.

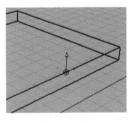

- In the Perspective window, click on the *edge* of the table using **Alt** + **Shift** and the **LMB**.

- Wait for a brief second, and then release the **LMB**.

  You should now see the point of interest appear, around which the Perspective view will tumble.

Point of interest

To turn the point of interest feature on or off, go to:

- **Studio** → **Preferences** → **General Preferences** → ❐.

- In the options, click on **Input** on the left side; and you will see a checkbox with the name **Use point of interest**.

Tip: *Try to use the **F5** through **F8** buttons on your keyboard, they will make your modeling windows full screen. **F9** resets the default layout.*

6 Creating two additional legs

Select the now inactive (blue) leg by dragging a box over it with the *left* mouse button.

- **Palette → Pick → Object.**

When selecting objects, the three different mouse buttons actually have different effects:

LMB = toggles (switches) everything inside selection box;

MMB = selects everything inside selection box;

RMB = deselects everything inside selection box.

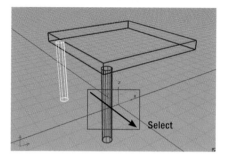
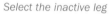

Select the inactive leg

Tip: *Make sure that you drag the selection box only over the inactive leg and no other parts of the table.*

Both legs should be white now (active).

- Go back to **Studio Edit → Duplicate → Object → ☐.**
- Click on the **Reset** button at the bottom of the window.

This will remove the number 5 that you previously entered for the Y-axis.

- In **Translation**, type **5** into the *first* column.

- Click on **Go.**

This will make a duplicate of both cylinders and move them 5 units in the X-axis at the same time, giving you four legs altogether.

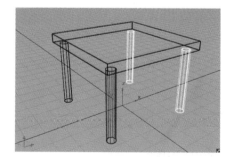

Duplicated legs

Lamp base

You will create a sphere for the lamp base. Deselect everything first:

- **Palette** → **Pick** → **Nothing**.

- **Palette** → **Surfaces** → **Primitives** → **Sphere** → ❑.

- In the options, set the number of **Sections** to **10** and click on **Go**.

- Click *once* anywhere in the *top* view to place the sphere.

Note: *If you click more than once, you will continue to place spheres.*

Scale and move the sphere to the top of the table:

- **Palette** → **Transform** → **Move** or **Scale**.

Notice how the different mouse buttons constrain movement or scaling relative to vertical or horizontal motion in the Orthographic views:

> **LMB** = no constraints;
>
> **MMB** = constrains horizontal movement and scale;
>
> **RMB** = constrains vertical movement and scale.

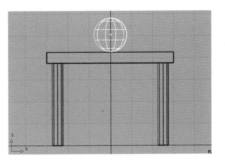

Move the sphere on top of the table surface

Moving CVs

You will now start modifying the **CVs** (control vertices) of the sphere to achieve greater detail.

With the sphere selected, go to the Control Panel on the right side of your screen:

- **Control Panel** → **Display** → **CV/Hull**.

- Click on the checkbox next to **CV/Hull**.

Control Panel

Lesson 01

Chapter One

Notice how you now see the CVs that hold the surface. The yellow color indicates that they are active and red indicates inactive.

You can pick a row of CVs, scale and move them:

- **Palette** → **Pick** → **Nothing**.

- **Palette** → **Pick** → **Point Type** → **CV**.

- **Click+drag** a box over a row of CVs in the *side* view (using the **LMB**).

- **Palette** → **Transform** → **Move** or **Scale** (using the **LMB**).

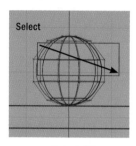

Select CVs

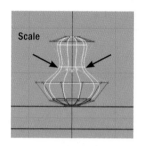

Scale CVs

Notice how the CVs scale relative to the pivot point. It is best to always select a row of CVs at once by **click+dragging** *a box over them.*

Tip: To make the CVs invisible again, uncheck the CV/Hull box in the Control Panel (with the sphere selected).

Lamp shade

Add a cone as a lamp shade the same way you placed the sphere:

- **Palette** → **Pick** → **Nothing**.

- **Palette** → **Surfaces** → **Primitives** → **Cone** → ☐.

- In the options, set the **Caps** to **0**.

- Click anywhere in the *top* view to place it.

- Use **Move** and **Scale** to position it as shown.

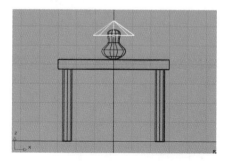

The finished cone for the lamp shade

Diagnostic shading

To see your model shaded without rendering it, try out the diagnostic shading options located in the Control Panel.

Select part of your geometry
and go to:

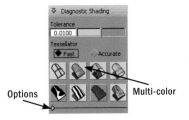

- **Control Panel** →
  Diagnostic Shading.

    Select any of the eight presets
    to see their effect on the
    model (the top left one will
    turn the shading off).

Diagnostic shading

Note: *Depending on the specific StudioTools package that you are working on, certain shading modes may not be available.*

Most commonly, you will be using the Multi-color (top row, 2nd from left) preset.

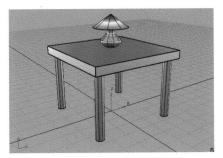

Table and lamp in diagnostic shading mode

Note: *Although very useful in evaluating surfaces, diagnostic shading is not always an exact representation of what the rendered geometry will look like. On large files, it can also slow down the system noticeably.*

Floor

Add a plane as a floor:

- **Palette** → **Surfaces** → **Primitives** → **Plane**.

- Type **0** in the promptline for its new position.

- Press **Enter**.

- Go to **Palette** → **Transform** → **Scale**.

- Type **40** in the promptline for its new scale.

- Press **Enter**.

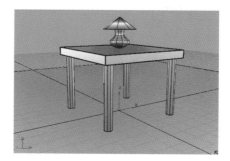

Table and lamp completed with floor

Tip: *To toggle the wireframe temporarily while in diagnostic shading mode, press the F12 button on your keyboard and review the results. To get the model back, press the F12 button again.*

Deleting

To delete any unwanted objects, select them first and then go to:

- **Studio** → **Delete** → **Del Active**.

- Confirm by clicking on **Yes**.

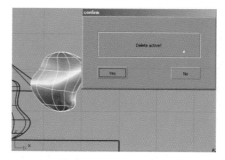

Delete extra geometry

Tip: *You can also use the Delete button on your keyboard.*

Lights

Now that you have created geometry, you need to add lights and color to the scene before you actually create a rendering.

Open up the Multi-Lister, in which you will create lights and shaders for the rendering:

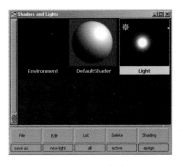

- **Studio** → **Render** → **Multi-Lister** → **List All ...**

Inside the Multi-Lister, go to:

- **Multi-Lister** → **Edit** → **New Light**

A new light icon appears next to the default shader.

Multi-Lister window

- Double-click on the icon to open the light parameter window.

In the window that opens, set the following light parameters:

Type = Spot;

Renderer Shadows = On;

Intensity = 16;

Shadow Color = pull the slider to about 75% gray;

Dropoff = 4;

Penumbra = 6 (make sure to also check the Penumbra box below).

Change the light parameters

Notice how the light is now visible as a spot in all views. It should still be active (yellow); if it is green (inactive), then select it first. Move the light about 10 - 15 units above the table and rotate it so that it is pointing at the lamp on the table:

Lesson 01

- **Palette** → **Pick** → **Object**;
- **Palette** → **Transform** → **Move**;
- **Palette** → **Transform** → **Rotate**.

Tip: *Place an additional 1-2 lights in the scene for better lighting results.*

Shaders

Now create a few shaders and assign them to the objects in your scene:

- **Multi-Lister** → **Edit** → **New Shader**.

With the shader icon active (white), select an object in your scene that you would like to assign the shader to and go to:

- **Multi-Lister** → **Shading** → **Assign Shader**.
- Open up the shader parameter window by double-clicking it.

  Set the following shader parameters:

  Shader Name = rename this with the name of the object;

  Shading Model = Blinn;

  Color = click on the gray field to open the color window.

- Repeat this process until all geometry has shaders assigned to them.

Click on Color to open the parameters

Now you should be ready to render your scene. Click on the top of the Perspective window to activate it and go to:

- **Studio → Render → Direct Render.**

Finished direct rendering

Tip: *In the direct rendering options, try both renderer and raytracer to see their different effects.*

Saving and restoring

When you save your work, it is automatically stored in your **Wire** directory. Try not to use the save function as you may accidentally overwrite a file you may still need. Instead, go to:

- **Studio → File → Save As.**

  Enter a new name and click on the Save button. Now delete everything:

- **Studio → Delete → Delete All.**

  This deletes everything, including your views. To open the saved file go to:

- **Studio → File → Open.**

- Double-click the saved file to re-open it.

Save your wire file

Rendering

To render a final image, you first need
to specify the size of the image and its
quality:

- **Studio** → **Render** → **Globals.**

  *Inside the Render Globals, set the
  following parameters:*

  Mesh Tolerance = 0.005

  Anti-aliasing levels = 4 and **16**

  Raytracing Maximum Limits =
  All to **2**

  Image File Output = 1280 x 1024

  *Close the window and start a
  rendering:*

Set the global rendering parameters

- **Studio** → **Render** → **Render.**

  When prompted, enter a name (this will be the name of the rendered image).

- Click on **Save** to start the rendering.

  *This will start the render monitor on the bottom left of your screen. To view
  the rendering click on the **Show** button.*

You may also look at the rendering by going to:

- **Studio** → **File** → **Show Image…**

  *This will open up your pix directory, in which all your rendered images are
  stored automatically. To view any file, simply double-click it.*

Marking menu

Using a marking menu is a fast and easy way to access all your favorite tools
and functions.

To access, hold down Shift + Ctrl and click on any of the three mouse buttons (MB).
You will see a series of pre-set tools appear radially around the location of your
cursor. Drag the mouse in any direction to highlight and activate that tool.

To customize your own marking menu, go to:

- **Studio** → **Preferences** → **Interface** →
  Marking Menus...

  Notice that the window has three folders, one for each MB.

  *To add a tool, simply select it with the **MMB** and drag into the Marking Menu window.*

  It will add it to the left side of whichever icon you drop it onto.

- To remove a function, drag it into the trash.

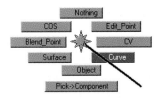

Marking menu

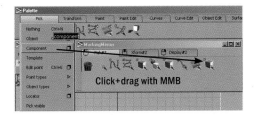

Adding tools to the marking menus

Tip: *Once you have customized all three buttons of your marking menu, you will be able to greatly increase your efficiency.*

Conclusion

In this lesson, you learned how to get started in StudioTools by modeling with primitive shapes and creating your first project. You created basic geometry, set their pivots, transformed them and even modified CVs. In addition, basic shaders were assigned and lights were brought out to render the scene.

In the next lesson you will learn more about the different rendering options, which will enable you to better understand the terminology and also help you create better and faster renderings.

Lesson 01

Lesson 02   Rendering options

*Now that you have created
your first scene, this lesson
will teach you some basic
features of the different
rendering options.*

In this lesson you will learn:

- The difference between raycasting and raytracing;

- How to set the Render Globals;

- The effect of Anti-aliasing;

- The effect of mesh tolerance;

- The effect of raytracing limits.

Raytracing versus raycasting

There are two main rendering options: **raycasting** (also referred to as *renderer*), and **raytracing**.

The **raycaster** is fast, and only gives rough shadows. Note that the shadows are approximate, and thus appear soft. Also note that the transparent sphere does not cast a shadow at all.

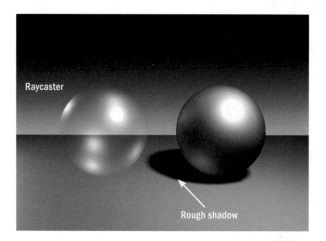

Rendered using raycaster

The **raytracer** takes substantially longer to render, but gives reflections, refractions and sharp shadows. Note that the transparent sphere now has a shadow as well.

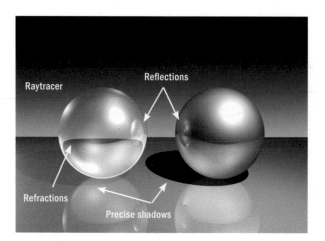

Rendered using raytracer

> **Note:** *The amount of reflectivity and refraction is determined by each object's assigned shader, while the properties of the shadow are controlled by the parameters in the light that shines on the objects.*

While reflectivity is nice, try to achieve a realistic effect rather than making everything shiny.

Render Globals

In the **Render Globals,** there are a few important options that can greatly increase or decrease rendering time, but also effect the quality of the final rendered image.

There are three presets, **Low, Medium** and **High.** Each changes the **Anti-aliasing Levels,** the **Mesh Tolerance** and the **Raytracing Maximum Levels** (only applies to raytracing; most of the time those numbers can be kept around 2-4).

The following sections show a close-up view of one of the spheres, illustrating the differences in rendering quality.

1   Anti-aliasing

When rendering with **Anti-aliasing** of **0,** the transitions between the edges of your objects will appear jagged. While this is not desired for a final image, it will render *much* faster this way. For all your test renderings, use **0 Anti-aliasing** to save time.

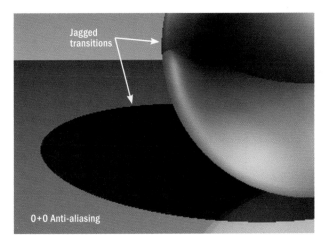

No Anti-aliasing

For final renderings, minimum and maximum **Anti-aliasing** of **9** and **16** is usually enough to produce quality results. Using higher numbers can dramatically increase your rendering time.

The image below was rendered using **Anti-aliasing** values of **12** and **25** to achieve smooth transitions between the shapes.

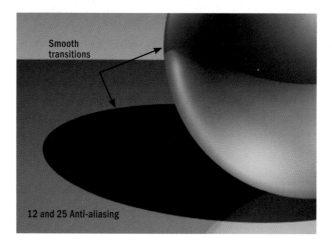

With Anti-aliasing

2 Mesh tolerance

When rendering, StudioTools divides every surface into a mesh of triangles. The **Mesh Tolerance** determines roughly the precision with which it renders the surfaces. The higher the tolerance, the faster the image renders and the more faceted it will appear.

The image below used a **Mesh Tolerance** of **0.1**; good enough for a test because it is fast but still able to display the shading and lighting correctly.

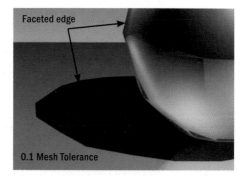

High Mesh Tolerance

For final renderings, you may have to lower the tolerance until it looks acceptable. Keep in mind that the tolerance you will need depends also on the settings in your construction options as described earlier.

A mobile phone modeled full-size may need a lower tolerance than a car modeled full-size.

The image below is rendered with a **Mesh Tolerance** of **0.005**, giving smooth edges along the surface outline and boundaries.

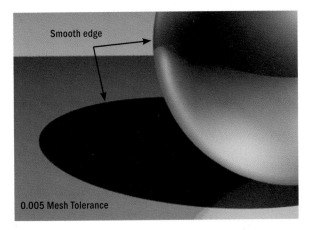

Low Mesh Tolerance

3 Raytracing parameters

In the **Render Globals**, the **Raytracing Maximum Levels** control how many times a light ray will bend (refract) in your rendered scene.

Take a look at the transparent sphere below. Notice that with the Raytracing Maximum Levels set to 0, the light does not penetrate the geometry.

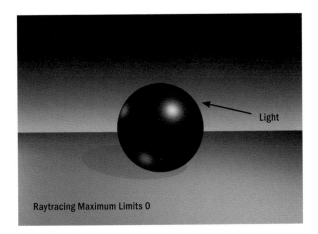

Light does not enter the geometry

With the **Raytracing Maximum Limits** set to **2**, the same sphere will start to appear realistic, as the light rays are fully passing through the geometry in two locations, entering and exiting the surface.

In most cases, this setting will deliver the most appropriate results while still keeping the rendering time low.

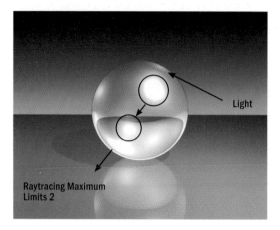

Light enters and exits the geometry

In the next rendering the **Raytracing Maximum Limits** are set to **4**. Notice how the light starts to bounce inside the sphere as well, adding additional refractions and reflections.

These or higher settings typically are only needed if you are dealing with multiple overlaying transparent objects. Higher raytracing maximum limits will greatly increase your rendering time and not necessarily improve the rendering quality.

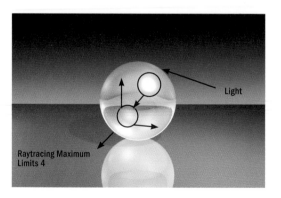

Light bounces inside the geometry

Conclusion

In this lesson, you learned the difference between raycasting and raytracing, and also how to understand and set the Render Globals for higher quality rendered images. In the next lesson, you will learn how to model with curves.

You are now ready for your first assignment to review the material covered thus far.

Assignment 1

Design, model and render a *unique* room using the tools and techniques learned so far. Try to add as much detail as possible including furniture, lights, interesting architectural details and also accessories. Render the scene full – screen (1280 x 1024 in the Render Globals).

STUDENT GALLERY > Next page

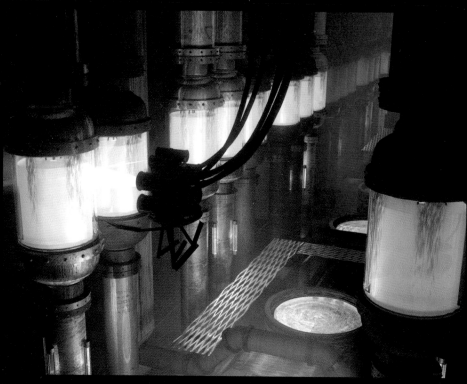

STEPHEN CHANG

"Stephen was going for a boiler room look and made great use of primitive shapes. Notice how the flying camera in the foreground is silhouetted against the brighter tubes, which adds an interesting negative shape. I especially like how he achieved depth by having a reflective wall in the background that acts as a mirror. The textures add a finishing touch to make the image look very cinematic."

JEFFREY JONES

"This is Jeff's concept for the ultimate DJ-club. I like how he maximized the simple loudspeaker geometry by duplicating objects and placing them everywhere, while still maintaining a very clean look. Notice that he achieved middle-ground by adding the stairs and nice subtle lighting from above."

Chapter Two >

Additive design

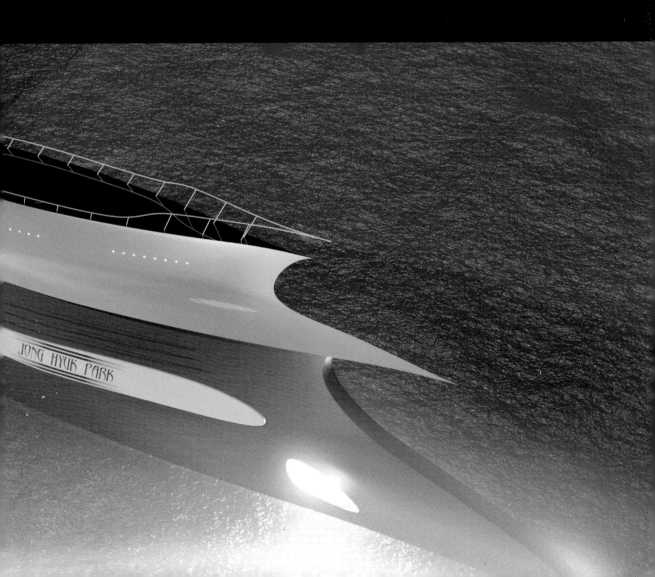

Lesson 03   Modeling with curves

*This lesson will teach
you how to create more
interesting and complex
forms and shapes by using
curves in combination with
basic surfacing tools. You
will use skin, revolve and
extrude in concise exercises
to become familiar with
their functionalities.*

In this lesson you will learn how to:

- Skin between curves;

- Use constraints;

- Revolve curves;

- Duplicate;

- Set planar;

- Extrude curves.

Skin

You can skin between any two or more curves to create surfaces.

1 Create curves

In the *side* view, create a new curve by going to:

- **Palette → Curves → New Curves → New Curves by CVs.**

  *Each time you click with the **LMB**, you will place out a **CV** (control vertex). By default, four CVs will create a curve, connected by a thin line called the hull.*

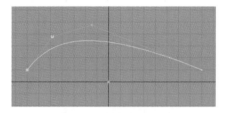

Side view of the CV curve

*After you have placed the first four CVs, use the **marking menu** to:*

- **Pick → Nothing.**

- Press **Shift + Ctrl** on your keyboard and use the **LMB.**

  Continue to place four CVs for the second curve.

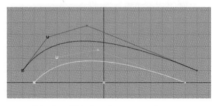

Placing CVs for the second curve

Note: *You did not have to go back to the Curve Tool to create the second curve.*

In the *Perspective* view:

- Select the smaller curve that you just created.

- **Move** it about four units on the Y-axis using the **MMB.**

  In the Perspective view, the three mouse buttons function as follows:

  LMB = move along X-axis;

  MMB = move along Y-axis;

  RMB = move along Z-axis.

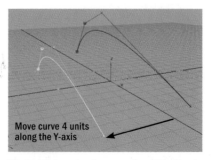

Move curve 4 units along the Y-axis

Moving the second curve along the Y-axis

Note: *Alternately, you could also use the promptline to enter the new position.*

2   Skin between two curves

You are now ready to create a skin surface between the two curves.

- Go to **Palette** → **Surfaces** → **Skin**.

  This will deselect both curves.

- Click first on the smaller curve.

  This will turn it white.

- Then click on the larger curve.

  This will create a skin in-between them.

- Use diagnostic shading to view the results.

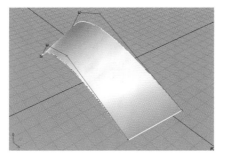

Resulting skin surface

The skin surface will have what is called **construction history**. Try to select one of the CVs and move it; you will notice that the surface will update accordingly.

Tip: *Whenever in doubt about how a certain tool works, look at the instructions in the promptline.*

Construction history is the relationship that the surface has to the curves that created it. As long as you do not modify the surface itself, changing any aspect of the curves will update the skin automatically.

3 Mirror

You will now duplicate the smaller curve across the XZ-axis so that you can skin between three curves.

- Select *only* the skin surface.

  Be sure not to select any part of your two curves.

- Delete the skin.

- Select the smaller curve.

- Go to **Studio** → **Edit** → **Duplicate** → **Mirror** → □.

- Select **XZ** as the **Mirror Across** axis.

- Click on **Go**.

  This will create a mirrored duplicate of the curve.

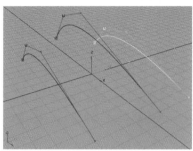

Mirror duplicate of the first curve

4 Skin between three curves

Go back to the Skin Tool and click on the first and second curve like before. The difference this time is how you select the third curve:

- **Palette** → **Surfaces** → **Skin**.

- Click on the first curve as before.

- Click on the second curve as before.

  This will give you the same linear skin surface as before.

- Hold down **Shift** on your keyboard and keep it pressed.

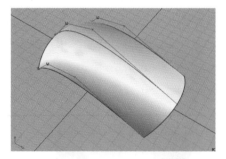

Skin between three curves

- Click on the third curve.

  Notice that the skin surface will make a smooth transition between all three curves, giving you a compound surface.

Note: *You can create skin surfaces between more than three curves as long as you keep the **Shift** key pressed.*

Constraints

In StudioTools, you can constrain an object's movement based on three parameters:

- **Snap to CV** (point);

- **Snap to Grid**;

- **Snap to Curve.**

    Use the following snap-to shortcuts on your keyboard:

    Snap to **CV** = **Ctrl**;

    Snap to **Grid** = **Alt**;

    Snap to **Curve** = **Alt** + **Ctrl**.

    Remember also that the three mouse buttons offer additional horizontal and vertical constraints in the Orthographic views:

    LMB = all directions;

    MMB = horizontal constraint;

    RMB = vertical constraint.

Try the following exercise to familiarize yourself with the different constraint options:

- **Palette** → **Curves** → **New Curves** → **New Curves by CVs.**

- Place the first CV using the **LMB** anywhere in-between the grid.

- Place the second CV using the **MMB**.

    Notice that you can only move it horizontally.

- Place the third CV using the **RMB** while holding down Alt.

    Notice that you can only move it vertically, and that it snaps to the grid.

- Place the fourth CV using the **MMB** while holding down **Ctrl** and clicking near the first CV.

    Notice how it horizontally constrains to that point.

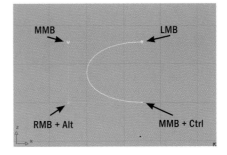

Constraints when placing CVs

Lesson 03

Revolve

You will create a curve using the constraint options learned in the previous exercise. Using the snap-to features will ensure that the revolve surface is accurate.

1 Curve on grid

While in the side view, go to:

- **Palette** → **Curves** → **New Curves** → **New Curves by CVs.**

- Place the first CV on the **Z-axis** with the **LMB** while holding down **Alt.**

This will ensure that the revolve will be closed on top.

- Place the second CV using the **MMB.**

This will ensure that the revolve has a smooth top without pinching.

- Place additional CVs to complete the curve.

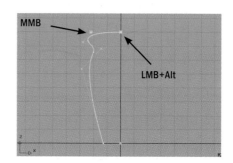

Curve to be revolved

2 Revolving

With the curve selected, go to:

- **Palette** → **Surfaces** → **Revolve** → ❑.

- Set the **revolution axis** to **Z** and the sections to **6.**

- Click on **Go.**

Notice the green arrow and the green line which let you interactively change the rotation amount and the tilt of the revolved surface.

If you get unwanted results with revolve, check to see if you set the revolution axis correctly, and that the original curve is actually along the Z-axis in the side view.

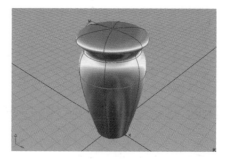

Completed revolve

Note: *Setting the sections to higher values will result in more accurate but larger geometry and subsequently longer rendering times.*

3 Curve off grid

In this next exercise you will sketch out another curve in the side view, but this time away from any axis.

- Place the first CV anywhere *in-between* the grid.

- Place the second CV above using the **RMB**.

- Place the third and forth CV *very* close to each other.

  Notice that placing CVs close to each other will start to pull the curve to a sharper radius.

- Place a fifth CV using the **MMB**.

  Notice that the pivot point is at the origin.

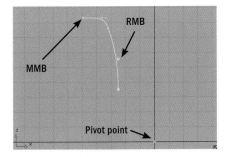

Curve off grid

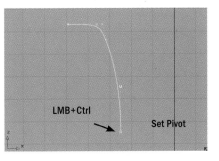

Pivot is snapped to the first CV

If you were to revolve the curve now around the X-axis, it would have a large opening in the middle because of the default location of the pivot. Before successfully revolving this curve, snap the pivot point to the first CV.

- Go to **Palette** → **Transform** → **Local** → **Set Pivot**.

- Move the cursor close to the first CV.

- Snap the pivot to the fist CV by holding down the **LMB** and **Ctrl**.

Lesson 03

If the pivot is on top of the first CV, you can revolve the curve with slightly different options:

- **Palette** → **Surfaces** → **Revolve** → ❐.

- Set the **revolution axis** to **X**.

- Click on **Go**.

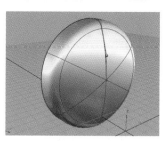

Finished revolve

Note: *It is important to have the second CV placed out perpendicularly to the revolution axis to avoid a pinch in the center of the revolve.*

Duplicate

The duplicate function can also be used as a modeling aid, especially if you transfer or rotate while duplicating.

1 Duplicating objects

Place a new sphere at the origin.

- Scale it down to **0.5**.

- With the sphere still selected, go to **Move**.

- Hold down the **Alt + Ctrl** buttons.

- Click on the original curve of the revolve using the **LMB**.

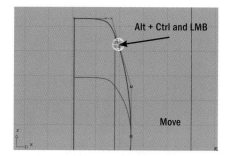

Place the sphere on the original curve

This will snap the sphere onto it and move it along its edge as long as you keep all buttons pressed.

Next, you will place the sphere's pivot to the center of the revolve. This is necessary so that additional copies of the sphere can be rotated around the shape. Go to:

- **Palette** → **Transform** → **Local** → **Set Pivot**.

- Hold down **Ctrl** and the **LMB**.

- Snap the sphere's pivot to the first CV of the original curve.

Next, go to the Duplicate Tool:

- **Edit** → **Duplicate** → **Object** → ❑.

- Enter **11** in the
  Number field.

- Under the **Rotation**
  field, enter **30** in
  the first column.

- Click on the **Go** button.

  *This will make eleven copies
  of the sphere around the X-axis,
  and it will rotate each copy by
  30 degrees.*

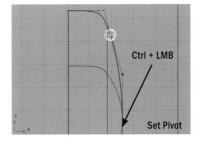

Set the pivot at the center of the revolve

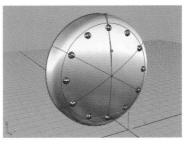

Finished duplicated details

2 Duplicating curves

Another method of modeling is duplicating curves off your existing geometry.

- Go to **Palette** → **Curve Edit** → **Create** → **Duplicate Curve**

- Click on the edge of the revolve.

  You will see a new curve appear.

- Move the duplicate curve along the X-axis with the **LMB**.

- Skin between the curve and the edge of the revolve.

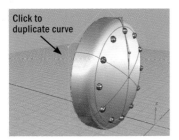

Duplicate curve

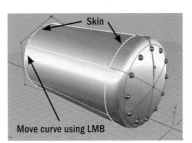

Skin between curves

Lesson 03

Note: *You can skin between curves and/or other geometry, making it a very fast and efficient modeling tool.*

Bolt

As you have seen in the previous exercise, with the placement of CVs you can also create the effect of rounded corners without using any advanced tools.

1 Creating the revolve

- Create a curve as shown in the image.

Remember to use the snap functions to constrain the CVs along the Z-axis.

Note how there are always two CVs placed very close to each other near the corners. The resulting curve is being pulled towards the corners, creating almost straight lines between small rounded edges.

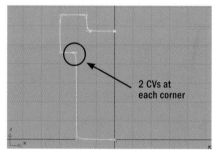

2 CVs at each corner

Bolt profile curve

Tip: *You can also snap two CVs on top of each other by holding down the **Ctrl** button while placing them.*

- Revolve the curve around the Z-axis with **12 Sections**.

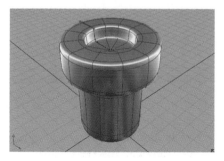

Rounded edges catch highlights

When turning on diagnostic shade, notice how the corners catch highlights, giving the object a more realistic effect without having to trim anything and without adding much geometry.

Note: *Although visually interesting and highly effective for rendering, this technique is not suitable for parts that are being modeled for rapid prototyping, because the resulting radius is not accurate.*

2   Rotating CVs

You can also achieve interesting effects by simply rotating CVs.

- Pick the original curve used for the revolve and delete it.

  You will be prompted if you want to delete the construction history – click yes.

- Use the control panel to make the CVs of the revolve visible.

- Go to the top view and select every second CV of the inside opening.

- Once selected, rotate them around the Z-axis.

  This will pull the surface towards the non-selected CVs, creating a hexagonal shape.

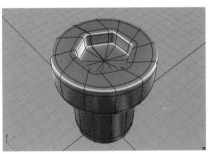

CVs to be selected   Bolt with rotated CVs

This method is great for quick indication of realistic detail, without creating unnecessary geometry. If the end result is sent to rapid prototyping, however, you should use some more accurate techniques as covered in Chapter 3.

Lesson 03

Extrude

To use the Extrude Tool, you must first create a profile curve and a path curve.

For the profile, use a primitive circle by going to:

- **Palette** → **Curves** → **Primitives** → **Circle**.

- Place it at the origin in the side view by holding down **Alt**.

   The profile curve is a cross-section of the final extruded surface and is perpendicular to the path at the origin of the grid.

For the path, create a new curve in the *top* view.

- **Palette** → **Curves** → **New Curves** → **New Curves by CVs**.

- Place the first CV at the origin by holding down **Alt**.

- Place the second CV along the Y-axis by using the **RMB**.

   This lines up the first two CVs 90 degrees to the circle.

- Continue placing additional CVs to complete the curve.

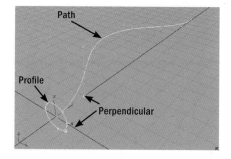

Profile and path curves

Now you are ready to extrude.

- Select *only* the circle.

- Go to **Palette** → **Surfaces** → **Swept Surfaces** → **Extrude** → ☐.

   In the options, note that you can create a start and end cap. For now leave them off.

- Click on **Go** in the options window.

- Click the **Go** button that appears in the lower right-hand corner to confirm the selection of the circle.

- Click on the path curve to create the extruded surface.

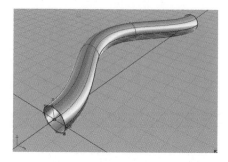

Extruded surface

Tip: *Instead of clicking the **Go** button, you can also press the **Space Bar** on your keyboard.*

Note: *If the two curves are not perpendicular to each other, you will get a flat-looking surface.*

I-beam

With the same techniques you can also create a realistic extrusion of an I-beam. This time, however, you will use three separate path curves to extrude to create a realistic 90 degree turn.

- In the *side* view, create a curve that will serve as the profile.

- Use *snap to CV* and *snap to grid* to place two CVs on each corner.

To create a realistic 90 degree turn, you will have to place three separate curves into the *top* view.

- Starting from the origin and using grid snap, sketch out a curve vertically along the Y-axis.

- Bring out a circle with the options set to 90 degrees, and place it as shown.

  In the example, it was scaled to 4 and grid snapped to touch the first curve.

- Finish by bringing out a third curve that also touches the circle.

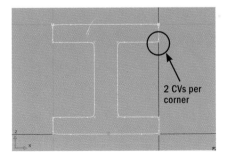

Profile curve for I-beam

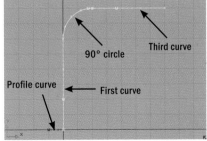

Three path curves

Lesson 03

- Use the **Extrude Tool** to create the first part of the beam.

- Then use its back edge of the resulting surface to extrude along the 90 degree circle.

- Use the edge of the circular extrusion as the profile for the last segment.

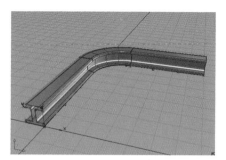

Finished extrusions

Note: *Although very fast and easy to use, the Extrude Tool has limitations in creating controlled surfaces.*

Set Planar

The Extrude Tool left the two ends of the surface open. To close these, you will use the **Set Planar Tool**. The Set Planar Tool lets you create a surface out of a closed curve, such as a circle.

- Go to **Palette** → **Surfaces** → **Planar Surfaces** → **Set Planar**.

- Click on the open edge of the extrude.

  You will see a menu that lets you choose between the curve or the extrude. You may select either one.

- Click on **Go**.

Set planar on the extrusion

Note: *The Set Planar Tool will only work with flat and closed curves, such as the ends of the extrude.*

LEARNING DESIGN WITH ALIAS STUDIOTOOLS

The Set Planar Tool also has the capability to create flat surfaces with holes punched out of them.

- Sketch out a new *open* curve as shown.

  Open means that the first and last CV do not touch and that the curve does not overlap itself.

- Go to **Palette** → **Object Edit** → **Close**.

- Click once on the curve.

  This will close the curve by connecting the first and last CVs.

- Create another curve *inside* the first one and close it as well.

- Select *both* curves.

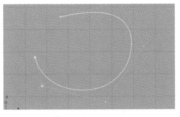

Open curve

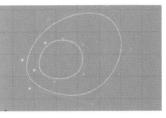

Two closed curves

- Go back to **Palette** → **Surfaces** → **Planar Surfaces** → **Set Planar**.

- Click on **Go** to confirm.

  Notice how this automatically creates a planar surface with a hole inside.

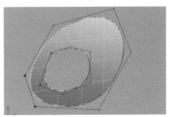

Completed Set Planar surface

Tip: *You can also have multiple holes in the same planar surface at the same time.*

Conclusion

In this lesson you learned how to get started using curves to create some basic shapes and surfaces. You now will use some of those techniques in the next tutorial to understand their implementation in a simple yet authentic workflow.

Lesson 03

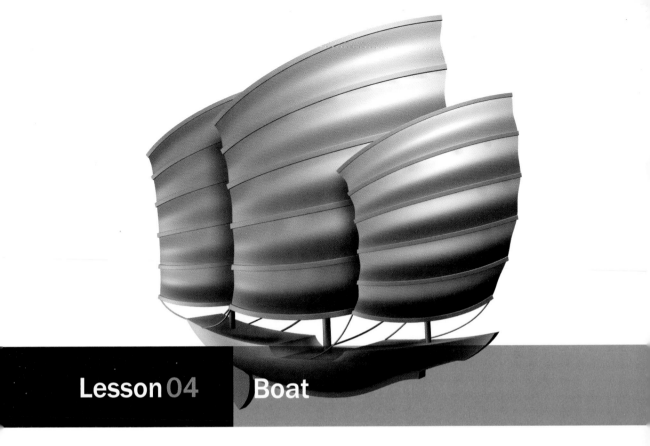

Lesson 04 Boat

In this lesson, you will take the previously learned tools and apply them to a boat to deepen your understanding of their functionality.

In this lesson you will learn how to:

- Create the boat hull using skin;

- Use the Object Lister;

- Insert isoparms, sections;

- Use patch precision, toggle template and toggle grid;

- Group and ungroup;

- Zero transform.

Boat hull

You will create the boat hull by sketching out one curve in the top view and then using duplicate and skin to create the surfaces.

- Create a curve by sketching it in the *top* view along the X-axis, using grid snap for the first two CVs and the last one.

  Try to use only five CVs and place the last CV so that it is about one grid unit away from the X-axis.

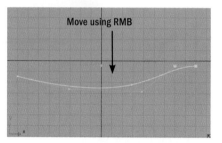

Curve for the boat hull

- Move the curve about a half unit down the Y-axis using the **RMB**.

  This will leave space for the keel line.

- Go to **Studio** → **Edit** → **Duplicate** → **Object** → ❑.

Move the curve slightly down

In the options, select three copies and enter the following numbers:

Translation	0	0	-0.25
Rotation	30	0	0
Scaling	0.9	0.9	0.9

Number	3		
Transform in	◆ XYZ space		◇ Geometry space
Translation	0.0000	0.0000	-0.2500
Rotation	30.0000	0.0000	0.0000
Scaling	0.9000	0.9000	0.9000

- Click on **Go**.

  By scaling and moving each duplicate, you will start to create a more dynamic effect than using revolve.

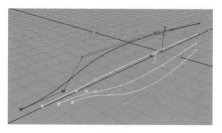

Three duplicated curves

- Go to **Palette** →
  Surfaces → **Skin**.

- **Shift+click** the four curves one-
  by-one, starting from the top.

  *This will create the new
  skin surface between
  the curves.*

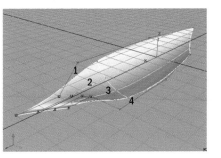

Completed boat hull

Object Lister

Notice that you can still see the CVs from the original curves. This indicates
that the four curves are still there, adding to the file size. To delete them, you
can select them either one by one in the Perspective view, or select them in
Object Lister:

- **Studio** → **Windows** → **Object Lister**.

  *The Object Lister is another way of
  looking at the objects in your scene.
  It can help you locate duplicate objects
  and plays an important role in grouping
  and ungrouping objects.*

- In the Object Lister, select the four
  items that are named *curve*.

- Use the **Delete** button to
  delete them.

Object Lister

Lesson 04

Keel

After you delete the four curves, you can insert more geometry close to the center of the boat to create the keel.

1   Adding an isoparm

- Go to **Palette** → **Object Edit** → **Insert**.

- Click+drag over the isoparm on the bottom of the boat hull.

  You will see a white line that you can move along the surface.

- Click either on the **Go** button or the **Spacebar** to confirm the position.

  By inserting an isoparm close to the bottom edge, you can create a sharp surface edge in the next step.

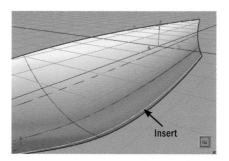

Insert isoparm

2   Moving a hull

When you now turn on the CVs, you will have greater control over the surface edge where you inserted the isoparm. Zoom in close and select the hull closest to the centerline. Note that there are two hulls next to each other.

- **Palette** → **Pick** → **Point Type** → **Hull**.

- Move it down the Z-axis using the **RMB**.

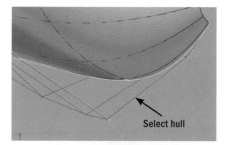

Select outside hull

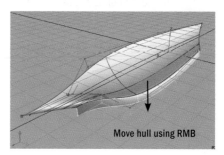

Move hull down

Finishing the hull

1 Mirror

Create a mirror duplicate of
your surface by going to:

- **Studio** → **Edit** →
  Duplicate → **Mirror** → ❑.

- In the options,
  select **XZ**.

  *This will make a mirror
  copy along the Y-axis.*

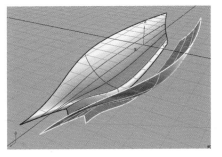

Duplicated boat hull

2 Close shapes

Skin across the top of
the boat shape. Instead
of using curves, click
directly on the edges.

Continue to close off the
remaining three edges
using the Skin Tool.

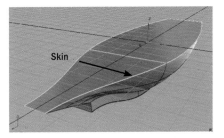

Skin between the two boat hulls

3 Add detail

Start to create a few more
skin surfaces by using
curves in the side window.

- Sketch out a total of six
  curves as shown.

  *Use the fewest amount
  of CVs possible to create
  the desired shapes.*

- In the top view, move the CVs
  of the curves as shown.

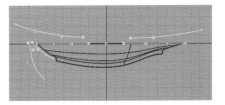

Six curves in the side view

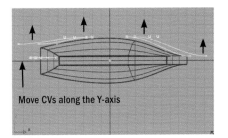

Adjusting the CVs

Lesson 04

Lesson 04
Finishing the hull

- Skin between the curves.

- Delete the six curves and make the CVs of the skin surfaces visible.

- Move the middle CVs to create some more dynamic shapes.

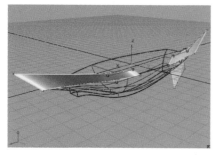

Resulting skin surfaces

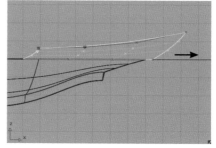

Move CVs

- Select the three surfaces and go to **Studio** → **Edit** → **Duplicate** → **Mirror** → □.

- In the options, select **mirror across** = XZ.

- Click on **Go**.

- Skin between all edges to close the shapes.

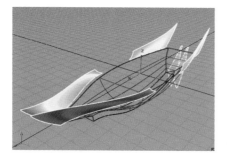

Mirror skins

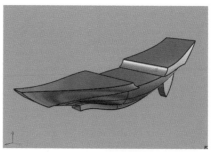

Finished boat with grid toggled off

Tip: *Toggle the grid for better evaluation by going to* **Studio** → **Display Toggles** → **Window Toggles** → **Grid**.

Mast and sail

1 Basic shapes

- Create a cylinder and scale it so that it will look like a mast.

- Sketch out two curves for the sail in the side view.

- Skin between the curves to create the sail.

- Delete the curves.

  This will also delete the construction history.

- Make the CVs of the sail visible and move them to create a more dynamic shape as shown.

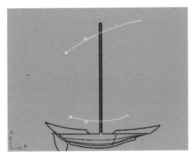
Curves for the sail

Adjusted CVs

2 Folds

Once the sail has been created, you can add more isoparms to modify the surface further. Instead of using the insert function, which would create inaccurate results, you will now use the Control Panel to adjust the spans of the surface.

- Select the sail.

- Type **10** in the second column of the spans sections of the Control Panel and press **Enter**.

  *The first column stands for the **U direction**, the second for the **V direction**.*

- Click **Accept** when the spans go horizontally.

Lesson 04

Lesson 04
Mast and sail

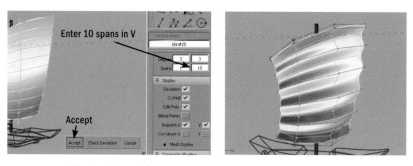

Adjusting the spans

Scaled hulls

Next, you select *alternating* hulls going across the surface.

- **Palette → Pick → Point Types → Hull.**

- Select every second horizontal.

- Scale them horizontally.

- Move them slightly along the Y-axis.

3   Cross beams

To create some extra horizontal beams that follow the shape of the sail, bring out a primitive circle with eight sections.

- Select alternating CVs and rotate them about 45 degrees, until they are on top of the unselected CVs.

  This will give you a profile curve that you can extrude along the sail's isoparms.

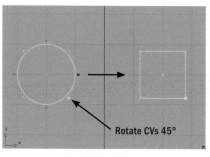

Rotate CVs

- Move the circle to the edge of one of the isoparms using snap to curve.

  Make sure it is rotated approximately 90 degrees to that isoparm.

- Using the extrude function, you can now extrude the profile along the isoparm.

  Repeat this process for all alternating isoparms to get consistency.

Once the sail is complete, delete all the curves you used to build it, and group all elements of the sail together. You can then duplicate the sail to create additional ones. Extra details can be quickly modeled using extrude, revolve and skin for extra ropes, railings, props, gears, water, etc.

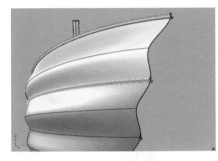

Extrude circle along isoparm

Completed boat

Patch precision

Once you have created a sea, you can select that surface and increase its **Patch Precision**.

- Go to **Palette** → **Object Edit** → **Patch Precision**.

- **Click+drag** in any of the windows to see the result.

Increasing the patches on any surface does not increase its geometry, but it is a helpful visual aid in evaluating your surface.

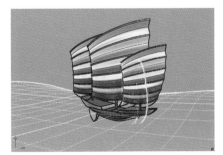

Patch precision

> **Tip:** The additional patches can also be used to extrude curves along, to duplicate curves from, or to skin to.

Template

Using templates can help to simplify your workflow. A template is visible in gray, but cannot be accidentally picked, and it also does not render. You can use it as an outline to create final geometry, or to hide parts of your model without making them invisible.

- Select some objects.

- Go to **Studio** → **Object Display** → **Template**.

To turn the template back into geometry, select it first by going to:

- **Palette** → **Pick** → **Template**.

  And then toggle it back with object display.

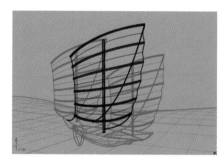

Toggle template

Grouping

If you want to group geometry together, select some objects first and then go to:

- **Studio** → **Edit** → **Group**.

  *Now open the **Object Lister** to see the hierarchy. Notice that all objects now reside under a new node. To select any of the parts, click on them directly in the Object Lister or choose them as components.*

- Go to **Palette** → **Pick** → **Component**.

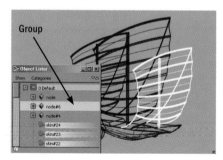

Grouping objects

If you move, scale or rotate a *group*, you are not actually changing any of the individual component values, but only the ones of the top node.

- Select the group.

- Go to **Studio** → **Edit** → **Ungroup** → ❐.

- In the options, choose **Delete Node**, and check **Preserve Position** to **Yes**.

  *If you choose **No**, the components will jump back to their original position, rotation and scale. Deleting the top node will get rid of the hierarchy that was created by grouping the objects together in the first place.*

Ungroup options

Tip: *If you have a component that you want to take out of a group without ungrouping everything, select it first and then use the **Extract** method.*

Zero transform

You can reset any object's rotation, move and scale values by using the **Zero Transform** function.

Select one of the duplicated sails, and open its **Information Window** by going to:

- **Studio** → **Windows** → **Information** → **Information Window...**

  In the transform info, you should see the sail's translate, rotate and scale information. On top, you can also enter a new name for the item.

Information window before

Lesson 04

- Go to **Palette** → **Transform** → **Zero Transforms**.

  Notice how all the information is being reset.

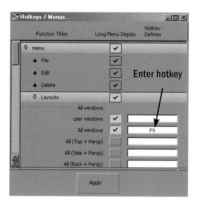

After zero transform

Hotkeys

At this stage, you may want to begin setting your own hotkeys to increase your productivity.

- Go to **Studio** → **Preferences** → **Interface** → **Hotkeys/Menus...**

  In the Interface window that pops up, you can set your own hotkeys for just about any function.

- Navigate to **Menu** → **Layouts** and *remove* **F9** for **User Windows**.

- **Enter F9** for **All Windows**.

- When done, click the **Apply** button to start using your own preferences.

  *If you are prompted to switch to Short Menus, select **No**.*

Setting hotkeys

Tip: *Setting* **hotkeys,** *as well as customizing your* marking menu, *will greatly increase your efficiency in using StudioTools.*

Chapter Two

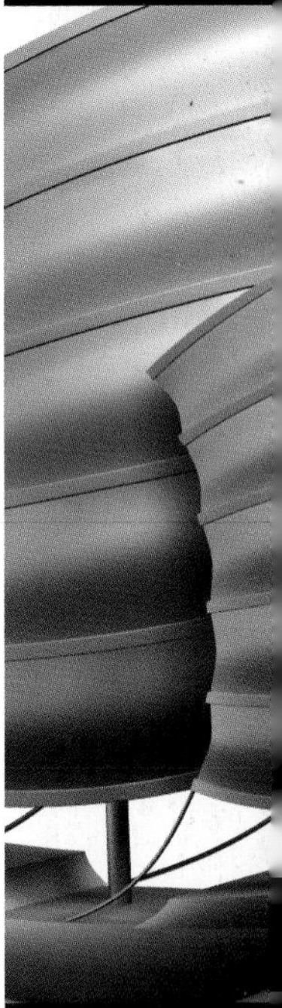

Conclusion

In this lesson you learned how to create some more interesting shapes with relatively simple tools. In addition to that, some technical information was covered to help you with your workflow. In the next lesson you will learn how to trim surfaces and create rounded edges.

Assignment 2

Using the new surfacing tools learned in this tutorial, design and build your own detailed sea vessel together with its respective environment and render it full screen.

STUDENT GALLERY > Next page

Lesson 04

TIM MEYER

"Tim's submarine was very successful due to its great proportions and beautiful lighting. Notice how most of the shapes are created with the Extrude and Skin Tools. I especially like the use of texture maps, which gives the vessel scale and realism. The windows were done with an incandescence map, and the lights have fog on them to create atmosphere."

ROBERT THOMPSON

Robert's boat has a dreamy feeling to it due to the pastel colors and interesting form. I like the overall composition with the two light rays shooting into the distance and the water trailing behind because it gives the image movement. Notice how the bright light in the distance is creating strong white areas on the surfaces like sunshine would do. This adds to the happy

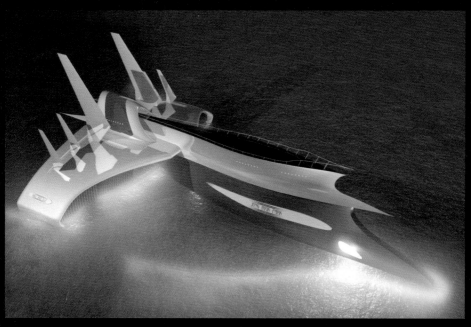

JONGHYUK PARK

"Jong worked very hard on this rendering and it paid off. I really like the dynamic shape and extravagant proportions of his boat, because it implies luxury and speed. The small railing on the top deck and the small windows give a sense of scale. Notice how he texture mapped his name on the side and the wing, adding extra detail to the whole image."

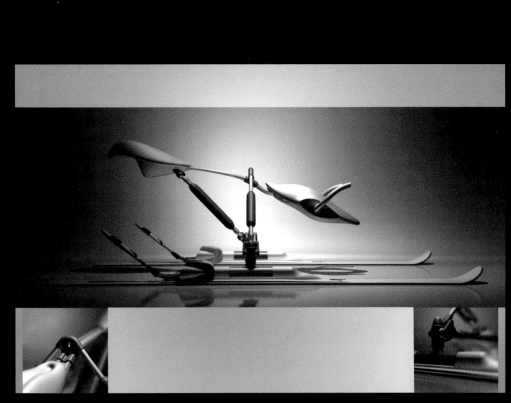

BRIAN WEN

"This image has a great overall look and feel due to its composition and industrial de-sign lighting. Notice how Brian used detail shots that have depth of field, giving them a photographic effect. He also used a seamless background with a spot light on it, which silhouettes his design and emphasizes the product's architecture."

Chapter Three >

Subtractive design

Lesson 05 — Trim and fillet

This lesson will introduce you to curves on surfaces, and you will use them to trim geometry and create rounded corners.

In this lesson you will learn how to:

- Create a curve on surface using the project feature;

- Intersect geometry to create curves on surfaces;

- Create curves on surfaces using geometry mapping;

- Trim and untrim;

- Trim divide;

- Multiple trim;

- Round surface edges;

- Use surface fillets.

Curve on surface

In order to trim a surface, you must first create a curve on surface, which will allow StudioTools to distinguish between areas that you would like to keep, and ones that you want to discard. As such, the curve on surface needs to clearly distinguish those areas, without having any gaps.

1 Project

In the *top* view, create a plane and curve that starts and ends outside of the plane as shown.

With the plane selected, go to:

- **Palette → Surface Edit → Create curves on surface → Project.**

  The plane will turn pink.

- Click on the curve.

- Confirm the selection by clicking on the **Go** button that appears.

  Notice the dotted red line around the edge of the plane. This indicates that it now has a curve on surface.

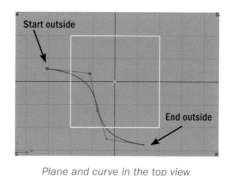

Plane and curve in the top view

Note: *Projecting curves onto surfaces works best in the Orthographic views. However, you can also project them in the Perspective view, but the result is based on the current position of the camera and is less predictable.*

- In the Perspective view, select your original curve on its edge.

- Move it slightly up in the Z-axis.

  Now you can see the curve on surface on the plane. Notice that it is going from edge to edge of the surface, which is essential for trimming.

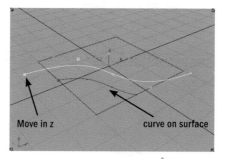

Curve on surface

Tip: *If you move your original curve in the X- or Y-axis, the curve on surface will update its position because it has construction history.*

Before trying out the next method of creating curves on surfaces, delete the existing one first. Select the curve on surface by going to:

- **Palette → Pick → Object Types → Curve on Surface.**

- Select and delete the curve on surface.

2 Intersect

Another method of creating a curve on surface is by intersecting two objects. By default, both objects will receive a curve on surface and the intersection location.

- Duplicate the plane used in the previous exercise.

- In the duplicate options, enter **Rotation 90** in the Y-axis.

- **Palette → Surface Edit → Create curves on surface → Intersect.**

  The vertical plane will turn pink.

- Click on the horizontal plane.

  In this case, the curves on surfaces are created without you having to confirm it.

- **Palette → Pick → Object Types → Curve on Surface.**

- Click on the intersect location.

  Notice how you will receive a choice of two curves on surfaces because there is one on each plane. However, they share the intersect location and thus appear as one.

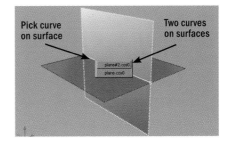

Two COS at the intersect location

Tip: *These curves on surfaces also have construction history. If you move either of the two surfaces, they will update their positions accordingly.*

Note: *You can only intersect surfaces, not curves.*

3   Geometry mapping

It is also possible to project curves onto a round or circular surface, such as a threaded cylinder or tire tread, using a tool called geometry mapping.

- Create a new cylinder in the top view.

- In the options, set the caps to **0**.

- Scale it to **2** and move it slightly away from the origin.

- Go to **Palette → Curves → New Curves → New Curve by Edit Points.**

- Hold down Alt for grid snap, and click once at the origin, and once at the first diagonal grid intersection.

  This will create a regular curve with four CVs that is perfectly straight.

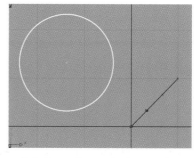

Cylinder and curve in the top view

With the cylinder selected, go to:

- **Palette → Surface Edit → Create curves on surface → Geometry Mapping.**

  It will turn pink.

- Click on the curve.

  This will map the curve onto the cylinder based on its geometry.

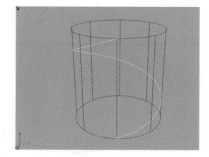

Geometry mapped curve on surface

The geometry mapping option window provides a further level of refinement, but in most cases you should be able to use the default settings as long as the curves are in the first grid quadrant.

Chapter Three

Trim

Now that you have learned two techniques for creating curves on surfaces, you have the prerequisite to start trimming surfaces. Begin by projecting a curve onto a plane as shown before.

- Select the plane.

- **Palette** → **Surface Edit** → **Trim** → **Trim Surface**.

- Click anywhere on the larger portion of the plane.

  Notice a cross bar that appears to confirm your selection.

- Click on the **Keep** button to execute the trim.

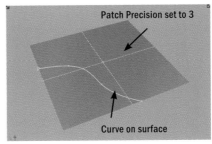

Plane with curve on surface

Now that the plane is trimmed, you will notice the **Revert** button that appears instantly.

- Click on **Revert** to undo the trim.

  This is a very useful feature as it quickly allows you to correct mistakes.

- Click on the crossbar and drag it over to the smaller area of the plane.

- Click on the **Keep** button again.

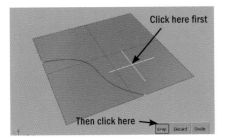
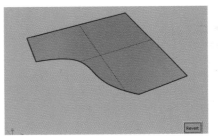

Select the area to keep   *Revert option*

Tip: You can also leave the crossbar in its place and try the **Discard** button instead.

Note: Trimming does not reduce surface geometry or rendering time. Instead, complex trims may actually increase both file sizes and rendering times.

Lesson 05

Trimming does not actually *cut* the surface apart, it only makes the trimmed area invisible. To see that the entire surface information is still available, including the discarded area, select the plane and make the CVs visible.

Trimmed plane with CVs visible

Untrim

The Revert button only appears right after trimming the surface. If at a later point you want to undo the trim, select the surface and go to:

- **Palette → Surface Edit → Trim → Untrim → ❐.**

  Notice that in the options you can choose to either undo the last or all steps. This becomes very useful if you have made a series of trims to a particular surface.

- Click **Go**.

  Notice that the entire surface is visible again, together with the original curve on surface.

Trim divide

Besides trimming, you can also do a **Trim Divide**, which will split the surface into two individual sections along the curve on surface. With the surface selected, go back to:

- **Palette → Surface Edit → Trim → Trim Surface.**

- Click on any section of the plane to place the crossbar.

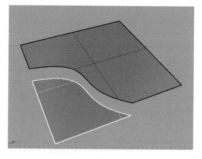

Trim divided surface

- Click the **Divide** button.

  Trim Divide actually makes a duplicate of the surface and keeps both regions, allowing you to assign separate shaders on each one individually.

- Select and move the two trim divided surfaces apart to see the effect.

Multiple trim

The **Trim Surface Tool** is also capable of projecting curves and trimming multiple surfaces at the same time. Untrim both planes from the previous exercise, place them next to each other and delete the curve on surface. In the top view, sketch out a new curve that will pass over both surfaces.

- Go to **Palette** → **Surface Edit** → **Trim** → **Trim Surface.**

- Click on the left plane.

  It will turn pink.

- Hold down **Shift** and click on the right plane.

  It will also turn pink.

- Release the **Shift** button and click on the curve.

  It will turn yellow, and automatically be projected onto the surfaces. This will now allow you to trim both planes.

- Click to place a crossbar on *each* plane.

- Click on **Keep.**

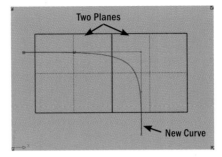

Two planes in the top view

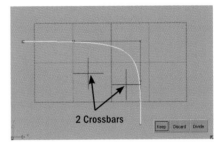

Place crossbars to select regions

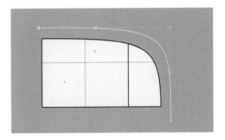

Trimmed planes without construction history

Note: *Unlike the* **Project** *and* **Intersect Tool,** *this method does not automatically produce construction history. If you move the original curve, the trim surface will not update. However, in the trim options you can select* **Projection History,** *which will give you the same effect as construction history.*

Round

There are multiple tools available to create a rounded transition between two or more surfaces.

1 Create two surface edges

Start by bringing out two primitives and intersecting them.

- Create a plane and scale it to **4**.

- Create a sphere and scale it to **2**.

- **Palette → Surface Edit → Create curves on surface → Intersect.**

- Intersect the two objects to create curve on surface.

    Notice that both the plane and sphere now have dotted red lines around their edges, indicating that they both have a curve on surface.

Proceed to trim both surfaces as before. With the plane selected, go to:

- **Palette → Surface Edit → Trim → Trim Surface.**

- **Keep** the outside area.

- Click on the sphere.

- **Keep** the bottom half.

    Notice that you can continue to trim without having to select the geometry first.

Now that you have created two meeting surface edges, proceed to use the Round Tool.

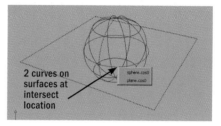

Plane and sphere intersected

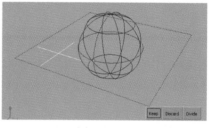

Keep the outside region

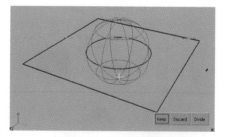

Keep bottom half

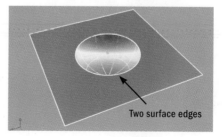

Trimmed geometry

2 Round edges

Whenever you have two surface edges meeting, you can use the **Round Tool** to create a smooth transition between them.

- Go to **Palette** → **Surfaces** → **Round Surfaces** → **Round**.

- Click once on the edge where the plane meets the sphere.

  Notice a white indicator showing the radius. You can change the radius either by **click+dragging** *the indicator or by entering a specific number into the promptline.*

- Set the radius to **0.5** and click **Build** to confirm.

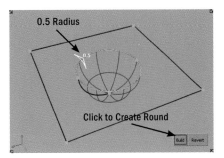

Set the round radius

The Round Tool will create a separate surface and simultaneously attempt to trim the other two accordingly.

The new round surface also has construction history, meaning it can easily be changed or undone.

- Select *only* the round surface.

- Go back to **Palette** → **Surfaces** → **Round Surfaces** → **Round**.

- Click on the **Revert** button to undo the round.

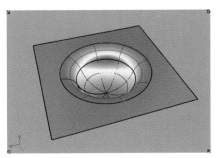

Round surface

Tip: *At this point you can also enter a different value for the radius and click* **Build** *again to see the result.*

3 Variable round

Instead of creating a round surface with a single radius, you can also specify a radius that will change over a specific distance.

- Create two planes that touch each other on one edge.

- Use the Round Tool to click on that common edge and make the radius **2**.

- Click again on the edge.

  This will create another radius of 2.

- Continue to place another two radius indicators with a size **1**.

  To move any of the indicators along the edge, click on the profile and use the **MMB***.*

- Click on the **Build** button.

  Notice how the resulting round surface is performing a controlled radius change as specified.

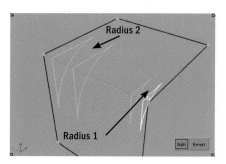

Four radius indicators

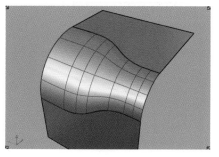

Variable round surface

Note: *Although the Round Tool is very powerful in creating sophisticated surfaces, it may fail occasionally. In that case, you may want to try the Round 9.0 or Fillet Surface Tool.*

Round & Round 9.0

You may have noticed that there are actually two tools with the same name: Round and **Round 9.0**. The 9.0 version is very reliable, but has limitations with complex edges. In contrast, Round can create those complex transitions with greater precision, but also has a tendency to fail on seemingly simple tasks.

1 Heart geometry

To learn more about the differences, create the following geometry in the top view:

- Create a plane and scale it to **6**.

- Sketch out a curve that is half of a heart shape.

- Snap the first and last CV to the grid using the **Alt** button.

- **Mirror** that curve across the **XZ-axis**.

Mirrored heart curve

- Move the two curves along the **Z-axis** above the plane.

- Make a duplicate of both curves.

- Move the duplicates straight below using the **RMB**.

- Create two skin surfaces between the curves.

- Intersect the two skin surfaces with the plane to create curves on surfaces.

- Trim plane and skins back so that the heart shape is cut out.

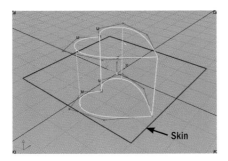

Skin between duplicate curves

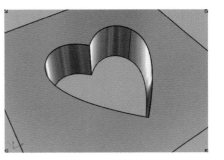

Trimmed heart

To see the limitations of the two Round Tools, you will use these shapes to try and create a radius along the top edge.

Lesson 05

2   Round 9.0

Make a duplicate of all three surfaces and move them to the side so that you can compare the results.

- Go to **Palette** → **Surfaces** → **Round Surfaces** → **Round 9.0**.

- Click on both the left and right edge of the heart.

- Use a small radius of **0.2** for this exercise.

- Click on **Build**.

  When using the Round 9.0 Tool, notice that it does not automatically close off the tip of the heart. As a result, the plane is also not trimmed back.

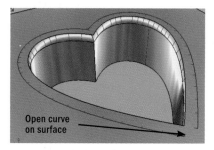

Round 9.0

When working with Round 9.0 you can use the **Toggle Extend Edge** option to close the tip of the heart.

- Select the round surface.

- Go back to the Round 9.0 Tool.

  This will open up the options again.

- Click on **Undo All**.

  This will revert the round surface.

- Click on **Tgl Extend Edge**.

  You will notice the edge line extending beyond the tip.

- Click on the opposite edge and repeat.

- Click on the **Build** button to see the result.

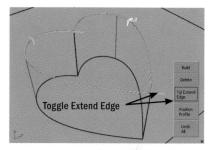

Toggle Extend Edge

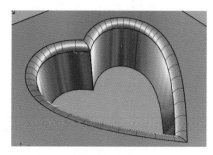

Round 9.0 with extended edge

Another way to use Round 9.0 is by first rounding off the edges of the heart surfaces by themselves. This would need to be done even *before* intersecting the plane, so that the plane can be trimmed correctly.

If you now round all *four* edges, you will see small additional surfaces added to perform the completed shape.

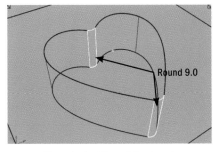

Rounded edges of the heart

Completed heart using Round 9.0

3 Round

The Round Tool will be able to complete the previous examples more efficiently. Use the duplicated surfaces for this exercise.

- Go to **Palette** → **Surfaces** → **Round Surfaces** → **Round**.

- Use the same radius of **0.2** on both edges.

- Click on **Build**.

  Notice that the Round Tool will be able to complete the desired surface, however, as mentioned earlier, it may have trouble with more complex surfaces.

You can also round over corners.

- **Revert** the previous round surface.

- Click on the two vertical edges of the heart.

  Choose a radius of **0.1**.

  Notice the two blue spheres at the intersections that indicate ball corners.

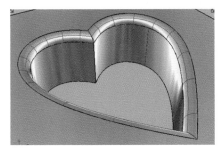

Round

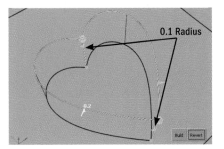

Add additional radius indicators

- Click on **Build**.

  *Notice that the ball
  corners created a more
  precise transition between
  the surfaces.*

Finished round surface

Surface Fillet

While both round tools are easy to use on simple geometry, the Surface Fillet
Tool can perform even better. Create another plane and sphere.

- Go to **Palette** → **Surfaces** → **Surface Fillet** → ❐.

- In the options, set the **Radius** to **0.1**.

- Leave the window open and click on the sphere.

  Notice the blue arrow that appears.

- Click on the arrow.

  *This will reverse its direction so that it points inwards. The arrow indicates the
  direction of the fillet surface.*

- Click on **Accept** when done.

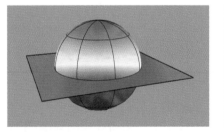
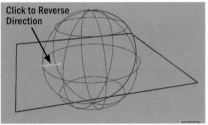

Plane and sphere   *Sphere with arrow pointing inwards*

- Click on the plane.

- Click on the arrow to make sure it points downwards.

- Click **Accept** when done.

  *Notice the resulting surface fillet that also automatically trimmed your objects.
  As long as you keep the options window open, you can also change the radius
  and click on the **Recalc** button to update the fillet.*

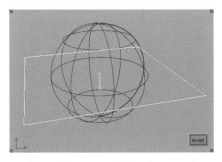

Plane with arrow pointing downwards

Finished surface fillet

Tip: *If the option window has disappeared, select the fillet first and then go back to* **Palette → Surfaces → Surface Fillet → ⬜.**

Variable Fillet

You can also create some very interesting variable fillets:

- In the option window, click on **Undo All**.

- Set the **Construction Type** to **Variable**.

- Click on the sphere, but this time have the arrow of the point *outwards*.

- Click on the plane, and have the arrow of the plane point *downwards* again.

- After accepting both selections, click on the edge to create another radius.

- Change that radius by typing **0.5** in the promptline.

Variable construction type

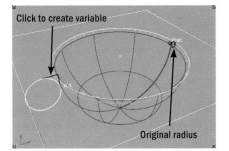

Change the second radius

Lesson 05

Lesson 05
Partlines

Tip: *You can move the new radius along the edge by using the* **MMB.**

- Click on the **Recalc** button in the options to see the new fillet.

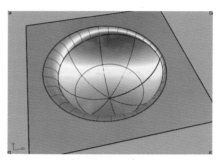

Variable surface fillet

Partlines

There are many different ways to create partlines in StudioTools. For simple geometry, you can use the Surface Fillet Tool from the previous exercise and just create an opposite part.

- Select all three objects.

- Group them together.

- Move the duplicate over to the side.

- Select the original surface fillet as a **Component**.

- Go back to **Palette → Surfaces → Surface Fillet → ☐.**

  This will open up the option window again because of the construction history.

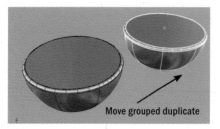

Move grouped duplicate

Select Component

Move the duplicated group to the side

Select original fillet

- In the options, click on **Undo All**.

  This will revert back to the original surfaces.

- Click on the sphere again, make sure the arrow is pointing inwards and click **Accept**.

- Click on the plane again. This time the arrow needs to point *upwards*.

- Click **Accept**.

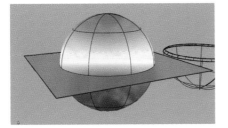

Reverted surfaces

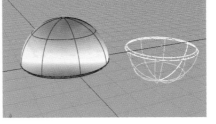

New surface fillet

- Select the part duplicated earlier and move it back to **0**.

  This will create the visual effect of a partline going around the sphere.

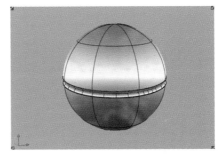

Completed partline

Conclusion

In this lesson, you learned all the main techniques for creating a curve on surface, as well as how to trim surfaces and how to round off edges. You are now ready to implement these new tools with the Wheels project in Lesson 6.

Lesson 05

Lesson 06   Wheels

In this lesson you will learn how to use the Revolve and Surface Fillet Tools to model wheels. You will create the rim and tire, and then apply shaders and textures to create a realistic effect.

In this lesson you will learn how to:

- Create layers;

- Create the rim;

- Create the wheel;

- Create spokes;

- Apply a tread pattern;

- Import Adobe Illustrator® files.

Layers

Before you start working on the wheel, create some new layers to better organize your file. Layers in StudioTools work similarly to ones in other software packages; they allow you to view/hide specific geometry, add symmetry, and keep your file nicely structured.

Start a new file and create a new layer by going to:

- **Studio → Layers → New.**

- Rename it *Curves* by double-clicking on its title with the **LMB**.

- Create an additional layer and name it *Wheel*.

    If the curves layer is active, as indicated by the beige color, then all newly created geometry gets assigned to it automatically.

- Click on the layer with the **RMB** to see its options:

    Visible = Toggles visible or invisible content

    Symmetry = Creates a mirror image of your geometry

    Assign = Allows you to assign active geometry to this layer

    Pick Objects = Picks everything assigned to this layer

Create new layer   *Layer options*

Rim

Start to create the rim by using the Revolve Tool.

1 Revolve

Create a new curve in the side view, which will be the cross-section of the rim. When placing the CVs, make sure that the first and second CVs are on the grid and are perpendicular to the X-axis by holding down the **Alt** key when you place them.

Note: *If you do not place the CVs perpendicularly, you will get a pinch in the center of your rim later on.*

- Go to **Palette** → **Curves** → **New Curves** → **New Curve by CVs**.

- In the *side* view, place the first CV at the origin.

- Place the next CV vertical on the Z-axis.

- Continue to place a few more CVs as shown.

- With the curve selected, go to **Palette** → **Surfaces** → **Revolve** → ❑.

- In the option window, set the **Revolution Axis** to **X**, the **Sweep Angle** to **60**, the Sections to **4** and click on **Go**.

This will create a section, which you will later duplicate to create a whole rim. Notice that the revolve is green, which indicates that it has construction history on it.

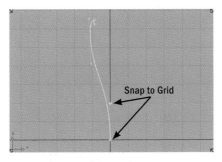

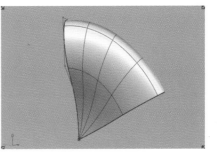

| *Curve for the rim* | *Revolved section* |

2 Skin

Create a curve in the back view, which will function as the hole that you will cut out of the revolve shape. Make sure the curve sits in the center of the geometry. The curve will have to be closed before you copy it to create a skin surface.

- **Palette** → **Curves** → **New Curves** → **New Curve by CVs**.

  Make sure the curve has no sharp turns, otherwise the Round/Fillet Tools will not work properly later on. Also, make sure that the last CV is not too close to the first one.

- To close the curve, go to **Palette** → **Object Edit** → **Close**.

- Click on the curve once.

  This will make a closed shape out of the open curve.

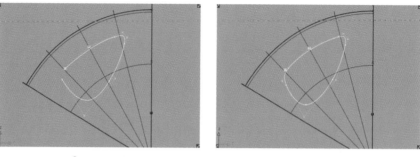

Open curve · Closed curve

- Duplicate the curve.

- Move the copy to the opposite side of the revolve so that you can skin in-between the curves.

If you want to create a tapered skin shape, you have to scale one of the curves smaller than the other. However, it will scale towards its pivot point, which in turn is located on the X-axis. To center the pivot before scaling, select the curve and go to:

- **Palette** → **Transform** → **Local** → **Center Pivot.**

  Now you can scale the curve and it will hold its relative position.

- Skin between the two curves.

Skin between the curves

3 Use layers

Start to clean up the model by selecting all the curves and assigning them to the curves layer.

- Go to **Palette** → **Pick** → **Component** → ❑.

- In the options, set **All** to **Off** and then check the box next to **Curves** and click on **Go**.

- Select over the entire model with the **LMB** and only the curves will get selected.

Pick component options

Tip:

Tip: *You should already have the Select Curves Tool in your marking menu, accessible with the* **LMB**.

- Click on the layer named **Curves** and with the **RMB** assign the curves to that layer.

- Turn that layer invisible.

- Repeat the process for the two surfaces, but assign them to the layer named *Wheel* and leave it active.

Next, select the objects and delete their construction history:

- **Studio** → **Delete** → **Delete Constr History**.

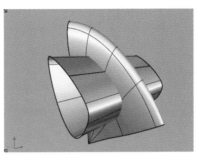

Deleted construction history

4 Fillet

Use the Surface Fillet Tool from the previous lesson to trim and round the edges between the two surfaces.

- Go to **Palette** → **Surfaces** → **Surface Fillet** → ◻.

- In the options, set the **radius** to **0.5**.

- Click on the skin and make sure the blue arrow points outwards.

- Click **Accept**.

- Click on the revolve and make sure the arrow is pointing towards the tapered end of the skin.

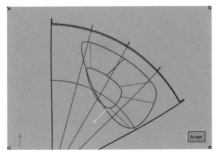

Fillet indicator on the skin

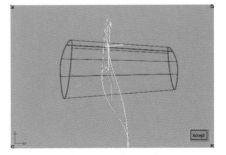

Indicator on the revolve

- Click **Accept**.

- Adjust the settings in the fillet options until you achieve the desired results.

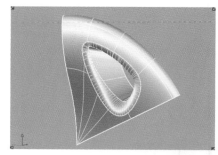

Finished section

5 Duplicate sections

At this stage, you could add more detail to the section by using the Round Tool. When done, select all elements and go to:

- **Studio → Edit → Group**.

Also, delete the construction history by going to:

- **Studio → Delete → Delete Constr History.**

Now that the three surfaces are grouped, you can duplicate the section to create a whole rim. Go to:

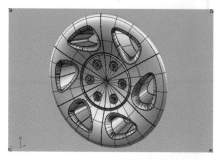

Finished rim

- **Studio → Edit → Duplicate → Object → ❐**.

- In the options, set the **Number** to **5**, the **Rotation** in **X** to **60** and click on **Go**.

This will make five copies, each rotated by 60 degrees, to create a full 360.

Note: *If you get a pinch in the center, your CVs were not aligned on the grid.*

6 Tire

- Create a tire by sketching a curve in the side view.

- Revolve it around the X-axis.

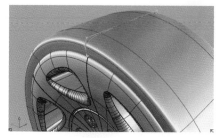

Finished tire

Chapter Three

Note: *Although it is possible to model the tire tread onto the tire using geometry mapping, the surfaces would be very complex. Instead, try to use a texture.*

Spokes

Using the revolve, skin and fillet techniques covered earlier, you can also create a rim with spokes.

1 Revolve

- In the *side* view, draw two curves as shown.

  Make sure that the lower curve is snapped to the grid, and that the second CVs are vertical to the X-axis.

- Revolve the two curves around the X-axis with a **36** degree **Sweep** and **4 Sections**.

  This will become one half of one spoke.

- Assign the two curves used to the layer called *Curves*.

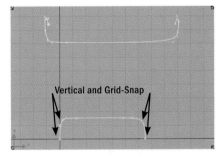

Two curves in the side view

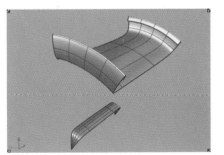

Two revolved surfaces

2 Skin

- In the top view, create one curve that will become the cross-section for the spoke.

  Make sure that the curve is visually within the smaller revolve so that they can intersect later. Also, make sure that the second CVs are again vertical to the X-axis.

Lesson 06

- Make two duplicates of that curve and scale them larger.

  This will give the spoke a more dynamic shape and form.

- Move the two copies up along the Z-axis as shown.

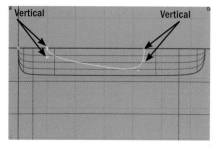

New curve in the top view

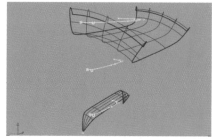

Three curves

- Create a skin surface through all three curves.

- Assign the three curves to the layer called *Curves*.

Intersecting surfaces

3   Surface Fillet

- Use the **Surface Fillet Tool** to create the transitions between the surfaces.

  In the following example, the **top radius** *is set to* **0.75** *and the* **bottom** *one to* **0.3**, *but you may have to experiment with different numbers to get the desired results.*

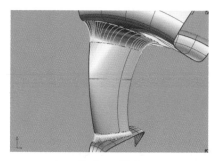

Surface fillets

Chapter Three

4 Duplicate

- Select all surfaces and mirror them across the **XZ-axis**.

  This will create a full spoke.

- Select *all* surfaces and group them together.

- Go to the **Duplicate Tool** to create the full rim.

- Enter **4** copies, each rotated **72** degrees in **X**.

- Create another revolve for the tire.

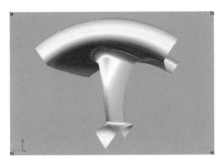
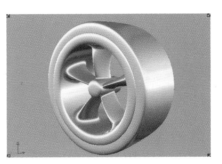

Full spoke   *Finished spoke wheel*

Tire tread

In a graphics program, create a square black and white texture that can be repeated, meaning top and bottom of the texture are the same. Make sure the file is *RGB* and saved as a *tiff*, *jpeg* or *Alias Pix* file into your **Pix** directory.

Tire tread texture

1 Assign the texture

- Open the **Multi-Lister** and assign a new shader to the tire.

- Double-click on the shader to open up its options.

- Go to **Special Effects** and click on the **Map** button next to **Bump**.

  This will open up the texture window.

- In the texture window, select **File**.

- In the File window, click on the Browse button.

This will lead you to your pix directory.

- Select the file of the tread that you created.

This will load it into the file and create a bump effect on your shader.

Select File

Browse for tire tread texture

2 Refine the texture

If you direct render now, you will see the texture being stretched across the surface looking very flat and undefined. You will need to adjust the texture placement and intensity in the file of the tread texture.

- Open the file and enter the following parameters:

    Intensity Amult = 0.4

    Blur Blurmult = 0.3

    Surface Placement V Repeat =5

    Chord Length = On

Chord length makes the texture spread evenly over the surface, without stretching over areas that have higher geometry.

Direct render of the texture

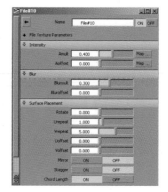

Texture options

If you test render now, your tire tread should look much better, but it will still wrap over the sides. To avoid that, you need to map a ramp onto the intensity of the file.

- Under the **Amult** of the **Intensity**, click on the **Map** button.

- Select a ramp in the texture window that pops up.

Adjusted rendering

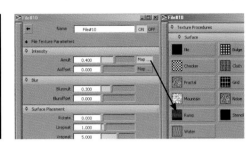

Select ramp

3 Adjust ramp

Change the ramp to a U ramp under Ramp Type, with a black bar on top and bottom and white ones in-between.

- To make a new bar, click anywhere in the color field.

- To adjust a bar's color, select it on the left round handle and then change the intensity below.

- To move a handle, select it on the round handle and move it up or down.

- To delete a handle, click on the right square button next to it.

The ramp will block out intensity of the texture on the sides, fading them to a smooth surface.

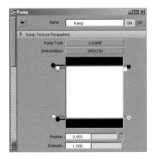

Adjust the ramp

Finished tread

Importing Adobe Illustrator® Files

It is possible to import an Adobe Illustrator® file, as long as it is exported as a legacy file version 8.0 or lower, and if it is outlined artwork.

To import typography, go to:

- **Studio → File → Import → File.**

  The geometry can be used to create surfaces or to project and trim them out of objects such as the tire.

Wheel with trim divided - Illustrator® text

Note: *You can also create similar effects with texturing as described in Chapter 5 of this book.*

Tip: *You can also try the text function under* **Palette → Curves → Text.**

Conclusion

In this lesson you learned how to apply the Revolve, Skin, Surface Fillet and Round Tools into building two different types of wheels. You also learned how to texture map the tire tread to create a realistic effect.

The next lesson will cover the Rail and Flange Tools, which enable you to create complex surfaces with greater detail.

Assignment 3

Using these new surfacing tools, design and build three different wheels and compose them together in one image rendered full screen.

STUDENT GALLERY > Next page

Lesson 06

CHAD DEJONG

"Chad's wheels have a very nice design and compostion. I like the unconventional treatment of the tire and the subtle color indication. Notice how the image leads you toward the center while bouncing off the right and left rims. The background also helps to bring the objects forward."

ROBERT THOMPSON

"Robert managed to make a very bold statement with his asymmetrical designs, detail and material indication. I like the fact that he added brake pad elements to create a strong level of realism."

BELLA CHU

"The set-up for this rendering is straight forward, but I love the Asian culture inspired design de-tails in the rims. Notice how Bella reused parts of the geometry of the middle wheel on the right one to quickly achieve a design variation."

PEI-CHIN SHIH

"Pei has a strong graphic design background and she really made good use of that in the design of her wheels. Notice the intricate flower details and beautiful negative shapes along with a few sparks of color that make these rims so unique."

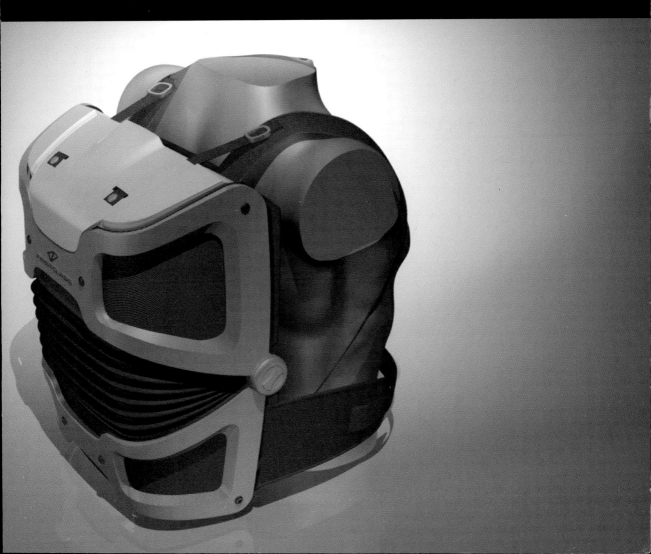

Lesson 07   Rail and rolled edges

In this lesson you will learn the different options offered in conjunction with the Rail Tool. The Rail Tool is incredibly powerful in creating a variety of complex surfaces and will become one of your primary modeling workflows. In addition, you will also begin using the Rolled Edge Tools, which are great for quick partline indication.

In this lesson you will learn how to:

- Interpret curvature;

- Create rail surfaces;

- Create a spring;

- Extend a surface;

- Detach and attach;

- Add CVs to a curve;

- Create a fillet flange;

- Use tubular offset;

- Create a tube flange.

Curvature

Note: *This feature may only be available in some versions of StudioTools.*

When sketching out curves, the placement and frequency of CVs will determine how clean the resulting surface will be and ultimately how geometry-heavy your file is.

- Sketch out two similar curves in the side view.

  Create the first one using only four CVs and the second one using as many CVs as you can.

To view the curvature of any object, select it and go to:

- **Control Panel → Display → Curvature U.**

  Click on the checkbox to activate it.

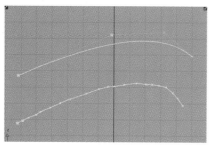

Two curves

Curvature in U

You will see some small lines and arrows showing the minimum and maximum radius of your curves. To increase the scale and samples, first click on the curvature properties located in the bottom of the control panel:

- **Control Panel → Display → Curvature Properties.**

  In the pull-up menu that appears, increase the scale and samples until you can clearly see the properties of each curve.

Take a look at the difference of curvature in the image. Notice how the top curve is nice and smooth, while the bottom one is very irregular.

If these curves were used to create surfaces, then the bottom one would result in a bumpy and messy object. Also, its reflection would be noticeably defective. In addition to that, the extensive use of CVs adds to the overall file size and causes longer rendering time.

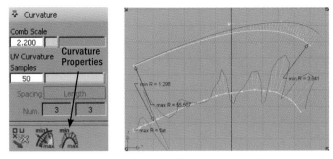

Curvature parameters   Curvature comparison

> **Tip:**   When sketching out curves, always try to achieve the cleanest result with the fewest amount of CVs possible.

Rail surface

The Rail Tool can create some of the most sophisticated surfaces, and over the next few exercises you will learn various options associated with it.

1   Rail curves

- Create two new layers.

- Name the first *Curves* and the second *Surface*.

- Sketch out a curve in the side view as shown.

Still in the side view, start a new curve that will be perpendicular to the first one.

- Place the first CV while holding down **Alt** + **Ctrl** and click on the curve.

  This will snap that CV onto the curve.

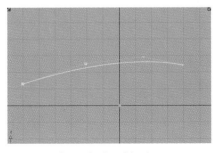

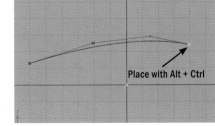

Curve in the side view   First CV in the side view

Lesson 07

Before placing the second CV, switch to the back view.

- Hold down the **MMB** to place the second CV horizontally from the first one.

- Continue to place two more CVs as shown.

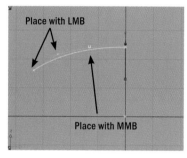

Second curve in the back view

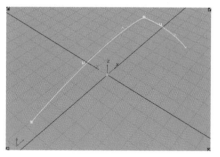

Two curves in the Perspective view

Note: If the two curves are not touching, the Rail Tool will not work. Also, if the CVs close to the centerline are not lined up horizontally, you will later get a seam in the center of your surface.

2 Simple rail surface

- Palette → **Surfaces** → **Swept Surfaces** → **Rail Surface** → ☐.

- In the options, set the number of **Generation** and **Rail Curves** to **1** and the **Continuity** of **Rail 1** to **Implied Tangent**.

  This will ensure that you get a seamless model when you use symmetry later on.

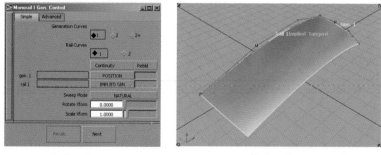

Rail options

Rail surface

- Click on the curve created in the *back* view first.

This will be the generation curve.

- Click on the second curve as the rail.

You will see a rail surface being generated.

Note: *Use implied tangency only for the centerline.*

3   Symmetry

- Assign the new surface to the layer named **Surface**.

- Under the layer options, turn on **Symmetry**.

  Symmetry in the layer options will give you a visual representation of the whole surface.

  To change the symmetry plane for an active layer, go to:

- **Studio** → **Layers** → **Symmetry** → **Set Plane**.

  *You will see a three-plane manipulator appearing at the origin, with the active symmetry plane indicator larger and yellow. To switch the symmetry, click on any of the two smaller inactive planes and click the **Set Plane** button.*

- Turn on diagnostic shading using **Horizontal/Vertical**.

- Make the curve layer invisible, so that you are only seeing the model.

  Check to see how the reflection of the whole surface looks, especially across the center.

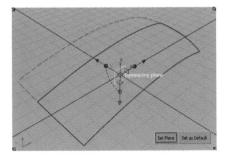

Symmetry plane

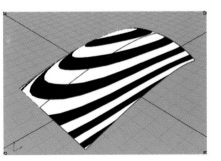

Check with diagnostic shading

4   Two generation rail

- Delete the previous surface.

- Make the curves layer visible again.

Lesson 07

- Create another generation curve that starts at the end of the rail curve.

   Try to give it a different characteristic than the first one and make sure to place the second CV horizontally.

- Go back to the Rail Tool options.

- Set the number of generation curves to **2**.

- Click on the two shorter curves first, then on the rail.

   You will notice a surface that has a much more controlled flow.

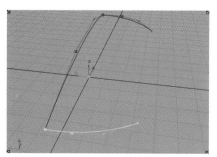
Second generation curve

Two generation curve surface

5   Two rail and generation surface

- Create another curve in the side view that will join the two generation curves together.

   Try to also give that curve a unique characteristic.

- Go back to the **Rail Tool**.

- In the options, set the number of rail curves and generation curves to **2**.

- Select the four curves as before and make sure the first rail curve is still the one on the centerline.

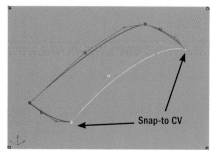
Second rail curve

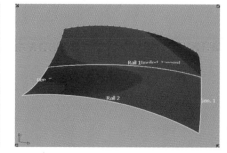
Two rail and generation surfaces

6   Multiple generation rail surface

- Add a third generation curve anywhere in-between the first two.

  For this curve, you must use snap to curve to place the first and last CV onto the rails.

- Go back to the Rail Tool and set the number of generation curves to **2+**.

- Select the three generation curves in succession as shown.

- Click the **Go** button.

- Click on the two rail curves.

  Notice that you will not get a result.

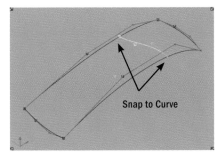
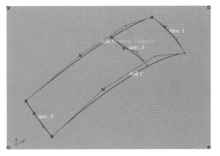

Third generation curve   *No resulting surface*

- Click on the button to the left of the promptline.

  This will open up the promptline history where you can see what may have caused the problem. Notice that StudioTools suggests to rebuild the rails.

- Go back to the Rail Tool options and click on the rebuild button next to the first rail.

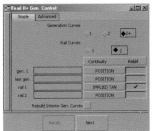

Promptline history   *Rebuild first rail*

- Select all three generation curves again.

- Click the **Go** button when done.

- Select the two rail curves.

This time you should receive a rail surface as shown.

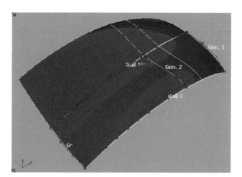

Completed rail surface

Using interior generation curves will allow you to create a variety of complex surfaces with great control over their flow.

Spiral

Another option of the rail surface is to have it rotate around its axis.

In the *top* view, create two perpendicular curves using edit points:

- **Palette → Curves → New Curves → New Curve By Edit Points.**

Creating a curve with edit points allows you to place perfectly linear curves by only clicking twice. Use the grid snap option for both curves.

- Go back to the Rail Tool options and set the **Rotate Xform** to **1800** degrees.

This will rotate the generation curve around the rail five times.

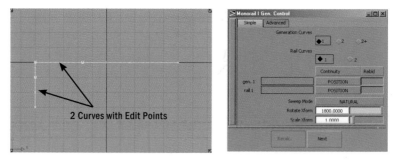

Two curves in the top view   *Rail options*

- Click on the generation and rail curve as before to create a surface.

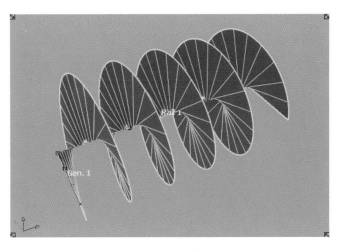

Spiral rail surface

Spring

- Bring out a primitive circle.

- Snap it to the outside CV of the generation curve.

- Scale it down as shown.

- With the circle still active, go to the **Extrude Tool**.

- Select the *rail* edge as the path curve.

  The result will be a coil surface that can be used as a spring or bottle thread.

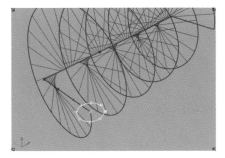

New circle on generation curve

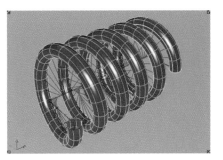

Coil surface

Triangular surfaces

You can also try to scale the rail surface either larger or smaller; the default is **1**. This can be used together or separately of the rotate option.

The following example shows a rail surface that has been scaled to **0**, making it come to a point at the end.

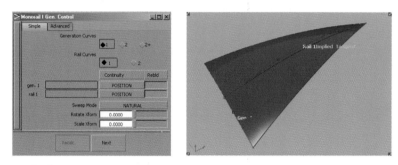

Scale set to zero

Triangular rail surface

> **Note:** *This technique works well for quick visualization, but is not necessarily suitable for rapid prototyping because the surface actually pinches at the tip.*

Extend

The Extend Tool allows you to continue a surface while keeping its original curvature.

- Go to **Palette → Object Edit → Extend.**

- Click on the edge of a surface.

- **Click+drag** until you achieve the desired result.

  In the extend options, you can also uncheck the **Merge** *box, which will then create a separate surface.*

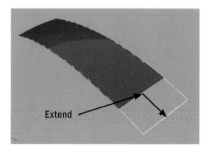

Extend Surface

> **Tip:** *The* **Extend Tool** *also works equally on curves.*

Detach

The **Detach Tool** allows you to split any untrimmed surface along its isoparms.

- Go to **Palette** → **Object Edit** → **Attach** → **Detach.**

- Click on any edge of a surface.

- **Click+drag** until you achieve the desired result.

- Click the **Go** button.

   The surface will be split into two at the specified location.

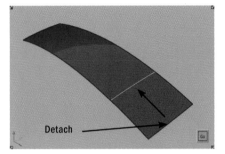

Detach Surface

Tip: *The Detach Tool also works equally well on curves.*

Attach

Although the Attach Tool also works on both untrimmed surfaces and curves, it sometimes produces unwanted results on surfaces. The following examples will use two curves to attach.

- Create two curves as shown.

- Go to **Palette** → **Object Edit** → **Attach** → **Attach** → ❐.

- In the options, choose **Blend** as the attach type and click on the **Insert Spans** and **Keep Originals** checkbox.

- Click **Go.**

- Click on the two curves near their gap.

Lesson 07

This will create a new curve that is blended together while at the same time the two originals are kept.

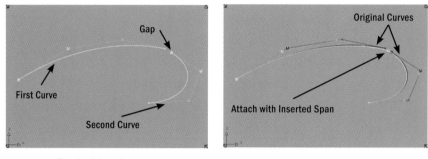

Two individual curves	Attach blend curve

Adding points

Another possibility for modifying curves is to add points.

- Select the last CV of an existing curve on *either* end.

- Go to **Palette** → **Curve Edit** → **Modify** → **Add Points**.

- Continue to click near the selected CV.

  Notice that you will be able to continue the curve with additional CVs.

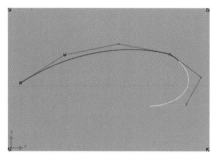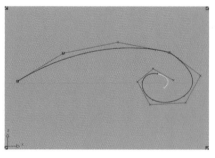

Select last CV	*Add CVs*

Rolled edges

Another method of creating partlines is by using the **Fillet Flange** and **Tube Flange** tools.

1 Fillet Flange Tool

Start by creating the following geometry in the top view:

- Create a closed circular curve and one that extends over the edge of a rail as shown.

- Project both curves onto the surface to create two curves on surfaces.

  You will use the circular curve on surface with the Fillet Flange Tool, the other with the Tube Flange Tool.

To use the Fillet Flange Tool, go to:

- **Palette → Surfaces → Rolled Edge → Fillet Flange → ◻.**

- In the options, choose a small **Radius** such as **0.05** and turn **Off** the **Create Flange** checkbox.

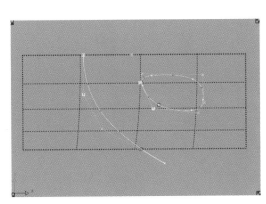

Project curves onto surface

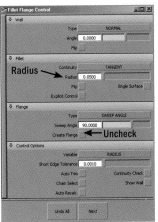

Fillet flange options

Tip: The **Create Flange** option would give you a wall, which can be useful if you want to create a true partline groove.

- Now click on the circular curve on surface.

  You will see a locator with a preview of what the radius will look like. If necessary, you can move the locator by clicking on the blue sphere. You can also change the radius in the fillet flange options window to see the effect.

- When done, click on the **Recalc** button to create the fillet.

  This will create the fillet. If the result looks satisfactory, you can now easily create the other side of the partline.

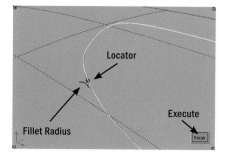

Fillet flange radius   *Created fillet*

- In the fillet flange options window, click on **Next**.

- Check the **Flip** box under **Fillet**.

Flip the next fillet

- Click on the circular curve on surface again.

  Notice that the fillet radius is now flipped.

- Click on the **Recalc** button.

  You will receive the second fillet, but this time it is on the opposite side.

Finally, since the Fillet Flange Tool already created additional curves on surfaces around its edges, trim away the gap between the two fillets to evaluate the result.

Opposite fillet   *Finished partline*

Chapter Four

2 Tubular offset

For the second curve on surface, you will use the Tube Flange Tool. First, you need to make a **Tubular Offset** of the curve on surface.

- Go to **Palette** → **Surfaces** → **Rolled Edge** → **Tubular Offset** → □.

- In the options, set the **Surface** to **None**, and choose a small radius such as **0.1**.

- Click on the curve on surface.

  Notice the blue preview of how the offset will look.

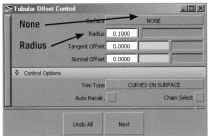

Tubular offset options

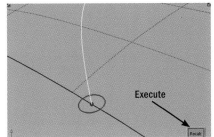

Tubular offset preview

- Click on the **Recalc** button to execute the offset.

  Notice that you will get two equally spaced curves on surfaces. These are essential for use with the Tube Flange Tool.

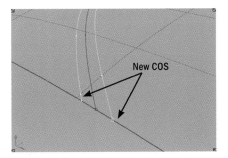

Tubular offset curves

3 Tube flange

- Go to **Palette** → **Surfaces** → **Rolled Edge** → **Tube Flange** → □.

- In the options, set the **Radius** to **0.08**, which is slightly smaller than the offset you created earlier.

This will leave a small gap, which is more accurate to a true partline.

- Set the **Sweep Angle** to **-270** and turn the **Flip** option beneath it to **On**. Check **Create Flange** and set the length to **0.05**.

- Click on your first curve on surface.

You will get a preview locator like before. Notice the small grey line at the end of the locator; this is the flange length.

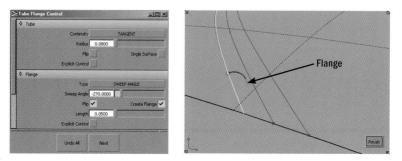

Tube flange options   *Tube flange locator*

- Click on the **Recalc.** button to create the new surfaces.

- With the tube flange option window still open, click on **Next**.

- Click on the second curve on surface.

  It is not necessary to make any changes in the options for this tool.

- Click on **Recalc** to create the second set of surfaces.

- Trim away the surface between the two fillet surfaces to evaluate the result.

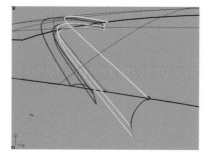
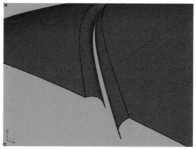

Tube flanges created   *Finished tube flange*

The main difference between tube and fillet flange is that the tube will give you a radius that is *on* the curve on surface, which is why you needed to first create the offset.

Conclusion

In this lesson you learned how to use the different Rail Tool options and also created two different rolled edges for partline indication. The next lesson will utilize some of the methods taught and apply them towards building a mobile phone.

Lesson 08   Mobile phone

In this lesson you will use all tools explored thus far to create a mobile phone. By now you have a variety of options on how to construct the volumes, and the following workflow is only one example to get you started.

In this lesson you will learn how to:

- Use rails to create basic surfaces;

- Project physical curves;

- Create a bevel detail;

- Use draft surfaces;

- Use offset surfaces;

- Project tangent;

- Add details.

Body

1 Top surface

Start by bringing out two curves and create a rail surface as shown in the previous lesson.

- Sketch the longer **Rail** curve in the *side* view.

- Snap the first CV of the **Generation** to that curve.

- Continue placing CVs in the *back* view.

  Make sure that the second CV of the generation curve is placed perpendicularly by holding down the **MMB**.

- Create a rail surface with implied tangency for the centerline.

- Create a new layer for the curves and turn it invisible.

- Assign the rail surface to a new layer and turn on symmetry.

  Make sure that there are no seams down the center.

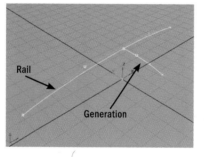

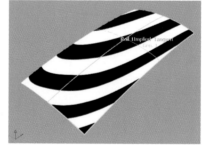

Rail and generation curves   *Rail with symmetry*

Next, turn on patch precision to better evaluate the geometry. With the surfaces still active, go to:

- **Palette** → **Object Edit** → **Patch Precision**.

- **Click+drag** anywhere in the window.

  The surfaces will get additional patches that do not increase rendering time, but help in evaluating the geometry. You can also enter numbers in the promptline to adjust the amount of patch precision.

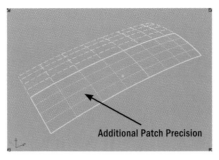

Additional Patch Precision

Patch precision

2 Bevel

To create a bevel detail, you will sketch out two more curves. These two curves will mark the width of the bevel.

- Sketch out two curves in the *top* view as shown.

Make sure that each of the first and last two CVs are lined up vertically from the centerline, and that they are within the rail surface.

Curves for the bevel

Tip: *If you sketch the curves on the layer that has symmetry on, you will get better visual feedback of what the complete outline will look like.*

- In the *top* view, select the surface and project the inner curve onto it.

The curve on surface that is created becomes part of the surface and you will later use this curve to trim the rail surface.

Lesson 08

For the second curve, you will change the options when projecting. Make sure you are back in the top view and go to:

- **Palette** → **Surface Edit** → **Create curves on surface** → **Project** → ⬚.

- In the options, select **Create Curve** and turn off **Match Original** and **Create History**. This will allow the newly created curve to have additional CVs so that it follows the shape of the surface better.

- Click **Go**.

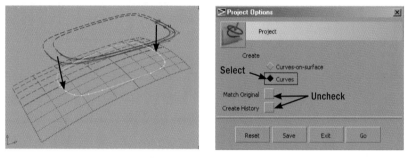

Projected curve on surface   *Project options*

- Click on the second outer curve in the *top* view.

  This will create a duplicate that follows the rail, but unlike the curve on surface, it is not attached to the surface, meaning you can move it around.

- Move the projected curve slightly down in the Z-axis.

  This will create more of an angle between the two curves.

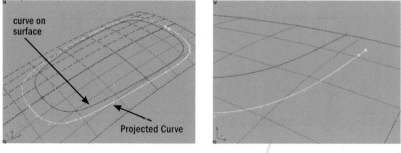

Projected curve   *Move curve down*

- Trim the rail surface, keeping the *inner* part.

  This will become the face of your product.

- Create a small curve that connects on both the edge of the trimmed surface and the end of the projected curve.

Use the snap-to functions to make sure the CVs touch both curves.

- Repeat the process for the other side as well so that you will have two generation curves.

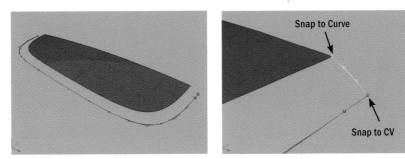

Trimmed surface   New generation curve

- Go back to the Rail Tool options.

  Change the number of rail curves and generation curves each to **2**, and make sure the continuity for the generation curves is set to implied tangent.

- Click on the small curves first, then the edge of the trimmed surface, and finally the projected curve.

Notice that the rail surface is distorted with many isoparms. This is caused by the trimmed edge.

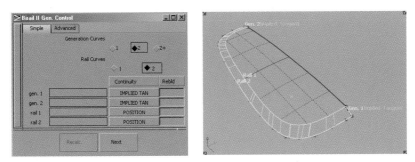

Rail options   Bevel rail surface

- In the rail options window, click on **Rebuild** for both rail curves.

Notice how the rebuild option optimizes the rail surface and creates cleaner geometry.

Rebuild rails

Rebuilt rail curves

3 Draft

Use the **Draft Tool** to create a surface from the edge of the rail.

- Assign all curves to the *curves* layer to make them invisible.

- Go to **Palette** → **Surfaces** → **Draft Surfaces** → **Draft/Flange** → □.

Leave the option window open.

- Click on the lower edge of the rail and confirm the selection by clicking the **Go** button.

You will immediately see a draft surface that is pointing upwards.

Draft surface pointing upwards

- In the option window, change the **Angle** to **180°** and make sure you have the desired **Surface Depth**.

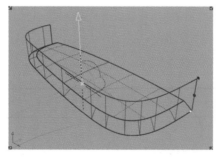

Draft options

The Draft Tool is a quick method for creating accurate linear surfaces.

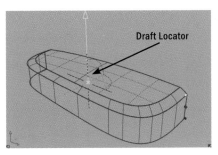

Finished draft surface

Tip: *Try to* **click+drag** *on the draft locator to interactively change the surface. You can also enter precise values into the promptline.*

4 Bottom

- Create a plane that intersects with the draft surface.

  Make sure that the plane fully intersects the draft, but that it only goes to the centerline.

- Use the Surface Fillet Tool with a small radius to create the bottom.

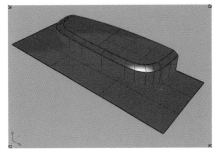

Intersecting plane

- Turn on symmetry on the surface layer to evaluate the finished shape.

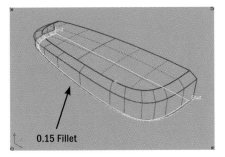

Surface fillet

Finished body

Lesson 08

Chapter Four

5 Screen

Select only the top surface and create an offset by going to:

- **Palette** → **Object Edit** → **Offset.**

- Use the **LMB** to adjust the offset distance.

- Click **Accept** when the green preview is slightly above the model.

Alternately, you can also enter a precise number for the offset in the promptline.

You now have a floating surface as shown. This offset surface will be used to create an additional raised detail to the design.

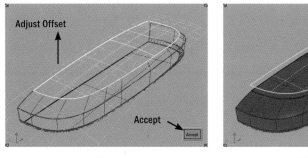

Adjust offset preview   *Offset surface*

In the top view, create two additional curves for the surface detail. These can be any freeform shape that you like, as long as the second CVs are perpendicular to the X-axis.

- Still in the top view, project the inner curve onto the offset, and the outer one onto the original top surface.

In the project options, remember to switch back to curve on surface.

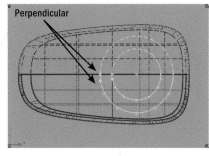

Screen curves

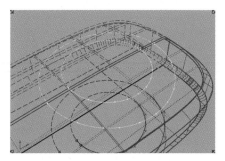

Projected curve on surface

- Trim out both surfaces so that you will get a small floating surface above the cut area beneath it.

- Create two more curves, snapping them to the edges of the trims.

  Try to create the new curves with edit points; that way, you only need to snap the first and last CVs onto the trimmed edges.

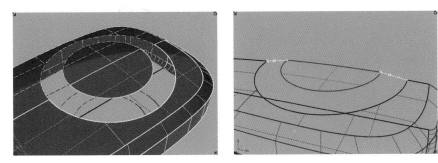

Trimmed screen area   Generation curves

To make the curves tangent to the surface edges, go to:

- **Palette** → **Curve Edit** → **Project Tangent.**

- Click on one end of the curve, then click on the edge of the surface next to it.

  The curve will bend to become tangent to the surfaces.

- Repeat the process for the other end of the curve and the other surface edge.

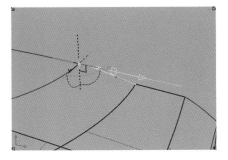 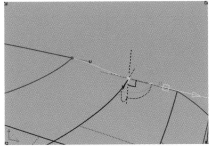

Project tangent   Project tangent on the other end

- Repeat the process for the second curve.

- Use the Rail Tool to create a surface.

  In the options, choose tangent for the continuity of the rail curves and implied tangent for the centerline. You may also have to use the rebuild option for one of the rails.

- Assign all curves to the curves layer and turn on symmetry to see the result.

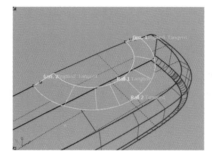
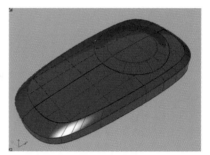

Tangent rail surface   *Finished screen*

6   Detail

Now that the basic shape is done, try to use the previously covered tools to create some refined details such as partlines, buttons, antenna, camera, etc.

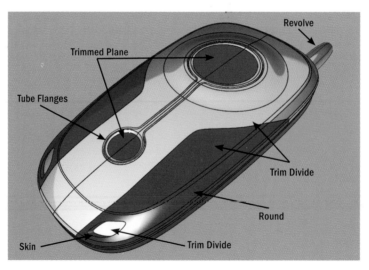

Finished details

Conclusion

In this lesson, you learned how to apply the tools introduced earlier onto a real project. In addition, you learned how to create draft surfaces and tangent surface details such as the screen area. The last step gave you a preview of the vast options of detailing possibilities, which you will now use towards the next assignment.

Assignment 4

Using these new techniques, design and model your own product and render it full screen. Pay attention to detail, clean surfaces and material/color indication.

STUDENT GALLERY > Next page

Lesson 08

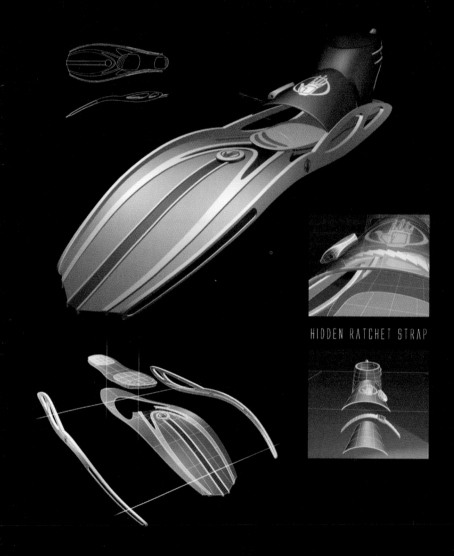

HIDDEN RATCHET STRAP

JEFFREY JONES

"In this image, Jeff used hidden line rendering techniques to enhance some of the additional detail views. I like how this creates a story between the small Orthographic views, the exploded views, and the final finished rendering."

NAIRI KHACHIKIAN

"Nairi modeled her mask and snorkel over an existing mannequin head. I like the use of multiple views to better describe the whole design. Notice how the curves of the mask have an even flow from all angles, and how there are no visible seams between the surface transitions."

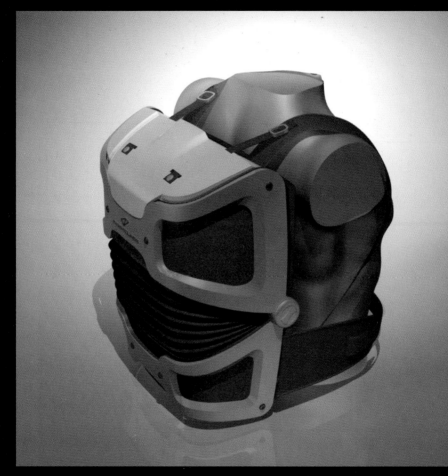

YOTARO TSUCHIYA

"Yotaro also made use of a mannequin to present his travel backpack. Notice how it has a halo around it, which is achieved by placing a spotlight against the seamless background. The detail and fabric indication were also very successful."

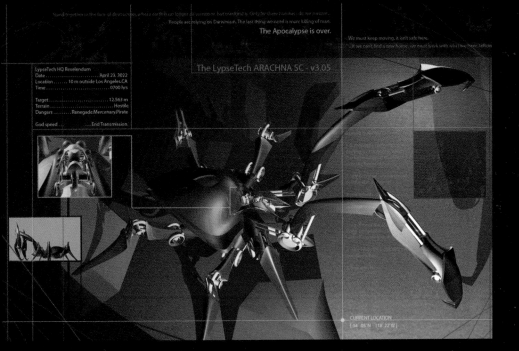

The LypseTech ARACHNA SC - v3.05.

LypseTech HQ Revelendum
Date . . . . April 23, 3022
Location . . . . 10 m outside Los Angeles,CA
Time . . . . 0700 hrs

Target . . . . 12.563 m
Terrain . . . . Hostile
Dangers . . . . Renegade,Mercenary,Pirate

God speed . . .   . . . End Transmission.

CURRENT LOCATION
(34 05 N   118 22 W)

CHUKRA CHARUHUNGSIN

I was really impressed by Chukra's work. He wanted to create an entertainment piece and I
challenged him into giving it a technical and graphic treatment. The result is a series of four
images, each filled with different views of details and call-outs. Well done!"

Chapter Five >

Texturing

Lesson 09   Camera effects

This lesson will introduce you to the various Perspective camera options.

In this lesson you will learn how to:

- Prevent clipping;

- Change the focal length;

- Twist and rotate the view;

- Use depth of field;

- Use image planes;

- Preview camera resolution;

- Use hidden line.

Camera Editor

1 Clipping

When working on close-up detail, the settings in the **Camera Editor** may clip away some geometry.

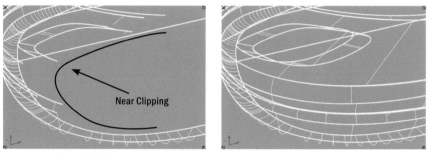

Camera with clipping   *Camera without clipping*

To fix this, make sure that you are in the Perspective view and go to:

- **Studio** → **Windows** → **Editors** → **Cameras...**

- In the options window, go to **Digital Properties** and set the **Near Clipping** to a lower number such as **0.1**.

You should now be able to zoom-in very close into your geometry without any clipping.

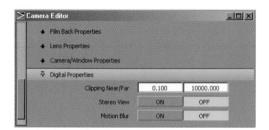

Change the near clipping

Note: *The Camera Editor will display whichever camera is active, including the Orthographic views. To switch between cameras, scroll to the top of the editor and see which camera is displayed.*

2   Focal length

While in the Camera Editor, you can also change the focal length.

- Under **Lens Properties**, change the number of the **User Focal Length**.

  A lower value will achieve a more wide-angle or "fish-eye" look; a larger value will create a more isometric effect.

Changing the focal length can enhance the look and feel, as well as the size and scale of your geometry and ultimately the rendered image.

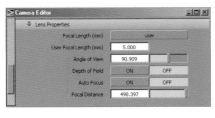

User focal length

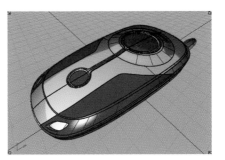

Fish-eye effect

3   Twist and rotate

You can also further manipulate the viewing angle of the camera in the viewing panel.

- Tumble in the Perspective view.

- In the viewing panel that appears, click on the two circular icons on the bottom to try out their effect.

  This will rotate the horizon and can sometimes help to create an interesting composition.

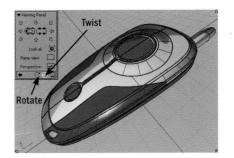

Twisting the camera view

4   Reset view

If you want to reset the view of any camera, go to:

- **Palette** → **View** → **Reset View.**

- Click inside any of the views.

  This will bring back the default view and is useful if the camera becomes too distorted.

Depth of field

Depth of field (DOF) can create some additional photorealistic effects, although it adds to the rendering time because it is a post effect. This means that the image will first be rendered normally, and the blur will be calculated *after* the image is done.

Place a few spheres in a row and make the camera visible by going to:

- **Studio** → **Display Toggles** → **Object Toggles** → **Camera.**

  *In the top view, calculate the rough distance from the **Eye** of the camera to the first sphere in grid units. The distance should roughly be 20 units.*

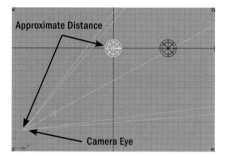

Calculate distance

- Go back to the Camera Editor and open the Lens Properties options.

  Set the **Depth of Field** to **On**, change the **F-Stop** to **8**, and set the **Focal Distance** to the number that you calculated as the approximate distance.

Tip: *The smaller the f-stop number is, the more DOF will be calculated. However, it also increases rendering times noticeably.*

To add default lights to the
scene, go to:

- **Studio → Render → Create
  Lights → Create Defaults.**

  *A directional and an ambient
  light will be created.*

DOF options

Note: *Default lights are ideal for quick lighting to render a test scene, however,
they are not useful for final renderings as the image will look flat.*

Make sure that your focal distance in the top view looks similar as shown.

- Direct render the scene in the Perspective view.

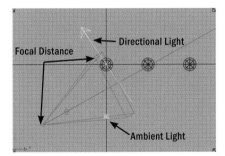

Default lights

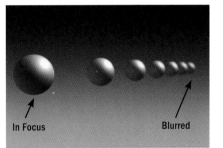

Depth of field

Tip: *Adjust the f-stop to a lower or higher value to see what effects you can
achieve with DOF.*

Lesson 09

Image plane

An image plane is much like a backdrop for your scene, and can be a quick and efficient way to complete an otherwise finished rendering. An image plane can be any **tiff**, **jpeg** or **Alias pix** file, however, it must be in **RGB** color mode.

1 Adding an image plane

Keep in mind that the size of the image plane should be the same as the size you intend to render. If you are rendering full screen, or 1280 x 1024 pixels, then make sure your image plane is at least that size or larger at 72 DPI, since that is what Alias is rendering at.

- Find a suitable image and save it as an *rgb tiff* file into your pix directory.

- Open up the Camera Editor.

Make sure that it is the Perspective camera and then click on **Add** under the **Image Plane** pull-down menu at the bottom.

This will direct you to your pix directory, in which you can choose the image saved earlier.

- Click on your image and then click on **Select**.

- This will load the image into the Perspective view.

Add an image plane

To move or scale the image plane, you must first select it by going to:

- **Palette** → **Pick** → **Object Types** → **Image Plane.**

Note: *Rotating an image plane does not work.*

If you now render your geometry, such as the wheel, you will see the image plane appear as the backdrop.

Wheel and image plane

Chapter Five

2   Use back color

When working with image
planes, you can also get
a shadow and a reflection
of your geometry into the
photo, tying the whole image
together. In the image,
notice the primitive plane
underneath the tire
that has been shaped to
follow the curvature of the
bridge in the image plane.

Curved ground plane

- Create a plane underneath your model.

- Assign a new blinn shader to it.

- Open the shader parameters.

- Under **Special Effects**, turn on **Use Back Color**.

  *The shader and the plane will now become the color of what is
  behind it – in this case, it is the image plane.*

By adjusting the reflectivity and matching the lighting situation, you
can achieve very photorealistic effects, as shown.

Use back color   *Raytracer with reflections and shadows*

Lesson 09

Previewing camera resolution

You may have noticed that the Perspective view sometimes crops the scene differently than when you render an image out.

To view the accurate camera resolution:

- Click on **Free** at the top of the Perspective window.

  A long pull-down menu will appear.

- Scroll down to one of the resolutions, such as render resolution.

Notice that your Perspective window will change proportions.

Render resolution

Hidden line rendering

A hidden line rendering will allow you to create an image of your wire frame.

First, adjust the parameters in the Render Globals:

- **Studio** → **Render** → **Globals...**

  Scroll all the way to the bottom.

- Open the **Hidden Line Rendering Parameters** tab.

- Change the **Hidden Line Parms** to **Global**.

- Set **Line Color** and the amount of additional **U** and **V Patch Lines** as desired.

Hidden line parameters

Next, create a direct rendering by going to:

- **Studio** → **Render** → **Direct Render** → ❑.

- In the options window choose **Hidden Line** as the **Renderer Type**.

- Click **Go**.

You will now receive a rendering that shows only the geometry – a very useful tool for evaluating surfaces and in conjunction with presentations.

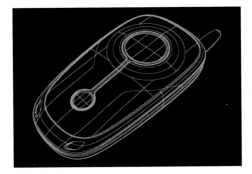

Hidden line rendering

Tip: *You can also make the background white by changing the environment shader in the Multi-Lister, so that you can, for example, sketch over the shapes.*

Conclusion

In this lesson you learned some of the powerful key features of the Perspective camera. You are now able to accurately compose your Perspective view in a variety of ways and enhance the output with image planes, depth of field or hidden line rendering.

In the next lesson, you will learn how to create shader effects.

Lesson 09

Lesson 10 — Shader effects

This lesson will introduce you to the various effects that you can achieve with shaders. You will learn how to interpret the different parameters and apply that knowledge in creating a variety of materials, including projecting logos onto surfaces.

In this lesson you will learn how to:

- Use shader types, shader and texture parameters;

- Create wire mesh texture, wood texture, carbon fiber texture, chrome texture, LED and LCD effects;

- Create stitching;

- Use projections;

- Layer shaders;

- Create clearcoat.

Shader types

There are four different shader types to choose from:

Lambert = *matte surfaces.*

Phong = *high-gloss/ shiny surfaces.*

Blinn = *semi-gloss surfaces.*

Lightsource = *cell shaded effects, does not emit light.*

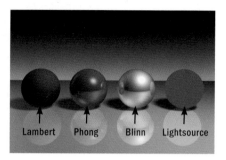

Four shader types

With experience, you will find that about 75% of all materials can be successfully created using **Blinn**, even matte and light emitting surfaces. **Phong** will be able to fill almost all remaining situations, including shiny materials such as glass, certain plastics and metals.

Shader parameters

Name of shader.

Changes the shader type.

Diffuses the highlight, good for plastics with some texture.

Color and intensity of the highlight.

Controls the highlight intensity at angled surfaces.

Controls the contrast between the surface and the highlight.

Controls how reflective the surface is (works only in raytracer).

Allows you to reflect textures into the surface, good to fake chrome.

Allows the environment shader to be reflected into the surface.

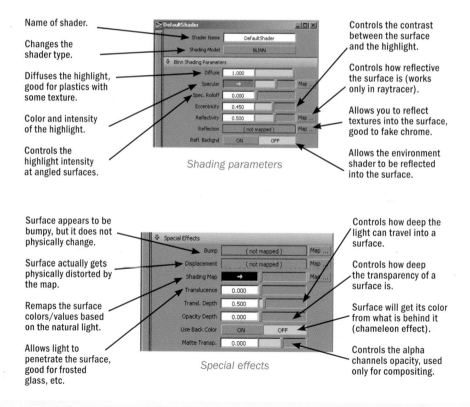

Shading parameters

Surface appears to be bumpy, but it does not physically change.

Surface actually gets physically distorted by the map.

Remaps the surface colors/values based on the natural light.

Allows light to penetrate the surface, good for frosted glass, etc.

Controls how deep the light can travel into a surface.

Controls how deep the transparency of a surface is.

Surface will get its color from what is behind it (chameleon effect).

Controls the alpha channels opacity, used only for compositing.

Special effects

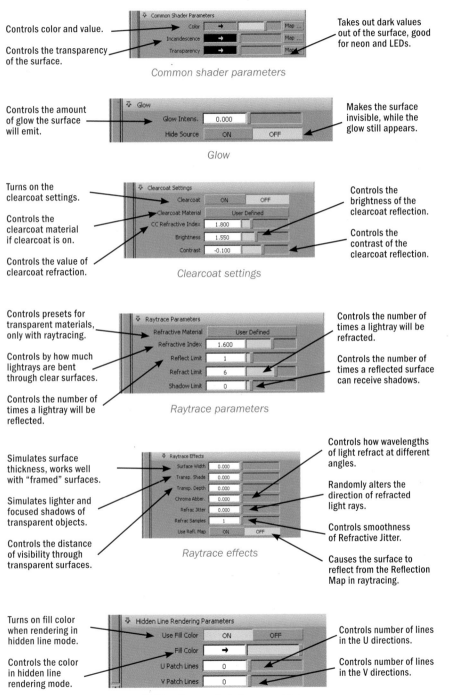

Controls color and value.

Controls the transparency of the surface.

Takes out dark values out of the surface, good for neon and LEDs.

Common shader parameters

Controls the amount of glow the surface will emit.

Makes the surface invisible, while the glow still appears.

Glow

Turns on the clearcoat settings.

Controls the clearcoat material if clearcoat is on.

Controls the value of clearcoat refraction.

Controls the brightness of the clearcoat reflection.

Controls the contrast of the clearcoat reflection.

Clearcoat settings

Controls presets for transparent materials, only with raytracing.

Controls by how much lightrays are bent through clear surfaces.

Controls the number of times a lightray will be reflected.

Controls the number of times a lightray will be refracted.

Controls the number of times a reflected surface can receive shadows.

Raytrace parameters

Simulates surface thickness, works well with "framed" surfaces.

Simulates lighter and focused shadows of transparent objects.

Controls the distance of visibility through transparent surfaces.

Controls how wavelengths of light refract at different angles.

Randomly alters the direction of refracted light rays.

Controls smoothness of Refractive Jitter.

Causes the surface to reflect from the Reflection Map in raytracing.

Raytrace effects

Turns on fill color when rendering in hidden line mode.

Controls the color in hidden line rendering mode.

Controls number of lines in the U directions.

Controls number of lines in the V directions.

Hidden line rendering parameters

Lesson 10

Texture parameters

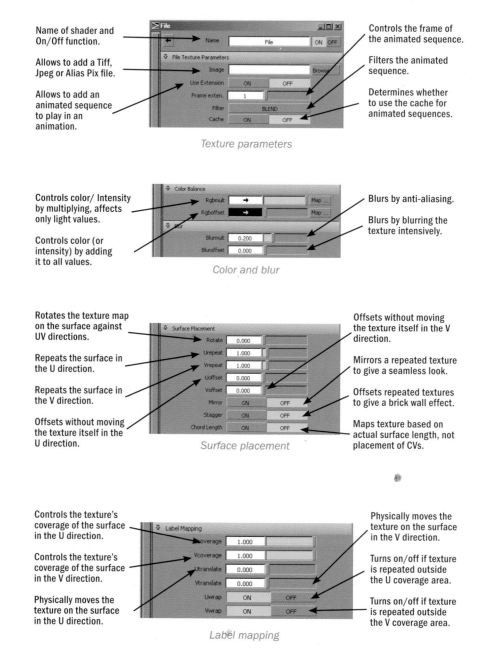

Name of shader and On/Off function.

Allows to add a Tiff, Jpeg or Alias Pix file.

Allows to add an animated sequence to play in an animation.

Controls the frame of the animated sequence.

Filters the animated sequence.

Determines whether to use the cache for animated sequences.

Texture parameters

Controls color/ Intensity by multiplying, affects only light values.

Controls color (or intensity) by adding it to all values.

Blurs by anti-aliasing.

Blurs by blurring the texture intensively.

Color and blur

Rotates the texture map on the surface against UV directions.

Repeats the surface in the U direction.

Repeats the surface in the V direction.

Offsets without moving the texture itself in the U direction.

Offsets without moving the texture itself in the V direction.

Mirrors a repeated texture to give a seamless look.

Offsets repeated textures to give a brick wall effect.

Maps texture based on actual surface length, not placement of CVs.

Surface placement

Controls the texture's coverage of the surface in the U direction.

Controls the texture's coverage of the surface in the V direction.

Physically moves the texture on the surface in the U direction.

Physically moves the texture on the surface in the V direction.

Turns on/off if texture is repeated outside the U coverage area.

Turns on/off if texture is repeated outside the V coverage area.

Label mapping

Inverts color and value of the texture.

Allows a second texture to be added to the mapping.

Allows for the original colors to be replaced (use with ramp).

Allows the texture to be altered by smearing, good to hide seams.

Makes a single pix file out of multiple overlayed textures.

Effects

Wire mesh

1 Set-up

Start by creating some simple geometry to use for this exercise.

- Create a primitive cylinder without caps.

- Assign a new blinn shader to it.

- Position a spotlight above the scene.

  Try to position the light so that it is approximately 90 degrees from the camera, bouncing off from the cylinder to create a nice highlight as shown.

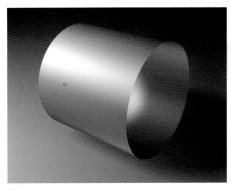

Primitive cylinder

2 Transparency

In the shader, go to:

- **Transparency** → **Map**.

- In the texture window that opens, select a **Ramp**.

Map the transparency

- Change the **Ramp Type** to **UV Ramp**, and the **Interpolation** to **None**.

Lesson 10
Wire mesh

- Bring out a total of four sliders, as shown.

  This will begin to create a mesh pattern.

- Set the following parameters under the surface placement to create a wire mesh:

  Rotate = 45

  Urepeat = 8

  Vrepeat = 8

  This will repeat and rotate the texture, creating more of a diamond shaped pattern.

- Direct render the scene to see the result.

  Notice how the transparent areas still catch highlights.

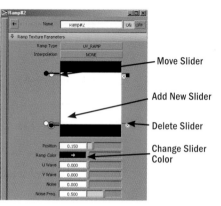

Ramp parameters

Move Slider

Add New Slider

Delete Slider

Change Slider Color

Surface placement

Note: *Raycaster will not give you shadows with objects that have transparency on them.*

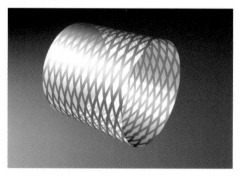

Transparency map

Chapter Five

3 Specular

You will need to save the ramp you just created for use on the **Specular** of the shader. With the **Ramp** selected in the Multi-Lister, go to:

- **Multi-Lister** → **File** → **Save As.**

- In the window that appears, enter a new name and click on the **Save** button.

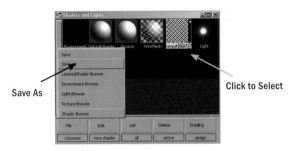

Save As

Click to Select

Save the ramp

Next, you need to reload the saved ramp into the **Specular** parameter of the shader.

- Click on the **Map** button next to **Specular**.

- In the texture window that will open, select the **Browse** button on the bottom.

Map the specular

This opens up your saved textures again.

- Select the ramp you just saved.

This loads the same ramp used for the transparency into the specular of your shader. If you render now, you will notice that the transparent areas have white highlights.

Browse for texture

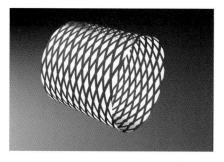

Cylinder with opposite specular map

To get the ramp to work properly, you will have to invert it.

- Click on **Invert** under **Effects**.

Invert ramp colors

- Direct render the cylinder to evaluate the result.

  The shader is using the same map for transparency and specular color. By inverting the specular map, you received the following effect:

  All areas that are transparent (white) will get a black (no) highlight.

  All areas that are opaque (black) receive a white (strong) highlight.

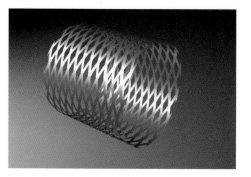

Correct specular map

4 Bump

To simulate thickness, you can reload the saved ramp into **Bump**. That map does not need to be inverted, but you need to adjust the texture parameters of the ramp.

- On the shader, click on **Map** next to **Bump**.

- In the texture window that appears, click on **Browse**.

- Reload the saved ramp.

- In the ramp, change the following parameters:

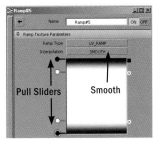

  Pull the two black sliders away from the white ones to create a smooth transition.

  Change the **Interpolation** to **Smooth**.

Adjust the ramp

  This will give you a gradient between black and white, which creates better bump results.

  Set the **Intensity Amult** of that map to **0.6**.

- Direct render the scene using the **raytracer**.

  *Notice that although the bump texture is giving the wire mesh a realistic feel, the transparent areas show distortion. This is caused by the shader's **Refractive Index**, which by default is treating it like glass. Also, notice that the cylinder is casting a shadow, but that it is not visible through the transparent areas.*

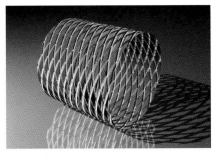

Raytraced cylinder

5 Refractive Index

- Open the shader and scroll down to **Raytrace Parameters**.

  Change the **Refractive Material** to **User Defined** and the **Refractive Index** to **1**.

  This will eliminate any distortion when raytracing.

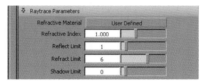

Change the raytrace parameters

6 Shadow Limit

To have the ground plane receive a shadow through the transparent areas of the cylinder, you will have to adjust the **Shadow Limit**.

- Assign a new blinn shader to the plane.

- In the shader, scroll down to the raytrace parameters.

- Change the **Shadow Limit** to **2**.

  This will allow the ground to receive a shadow through two transparent surfaces.

Shadow limit

- Direct render the scene again to evaluate the results.

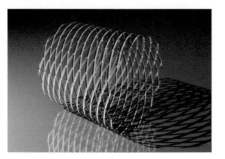

Completed wire mesh texture

7 Hardware shade

Another useful method of previewing your textures is using the **Toggle Shade** feature.

Go to **Studio** → **Display Toggles** → **Hardware Shade** → ❐.

In the options window, you have a variety of parameters to adjust the quality of display.

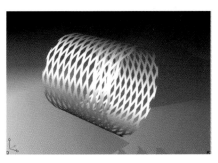

Hardware shade

Wood

The key to creating a successful looking texture is to start with a good image or photo. Depending on the level of detail and how close the texture will be to the Perspective camera, you need to scan the image at a relatively good quality, but try not to exceed approximately 1.5 MB, as this will add to your rendering time as well. Also, remember to convert each image to either **tiff**, **jpeg** or **Alias pix** files first, and make sure they are in **RGB** color mode.

1 Color map

- Save an image into your **Pix** directory.

Tip: *Create two folders in your pix directory, one that stores color and one that stores b/w textures.*

- Create a new blinn shader and assign it to the cylinder.
- Click on the **Map** button next to **Color**.

Wood texture

- In the texture window that pops up, select **File**.
- Inside the file, click on the Browse button next to Image.

  This will direct you to your pix directory.

Select file   *Browse for image*

- Select the saved image to be used as a color map.

  When you now render the image, your texture may appear distorted as it stretches around the cylinder.

Wood color map

To avoid stretching, repeat the texture using the Repeat U or V function until the scale of the texture looks appropriate. To achieve a more seamless tiling, you can try to use the Mirror function.

- If your texture is a horizontal format, as shown in the example, you can set the following parameters:

    Rotate = 90

    Vrepeat = 2

    Mirror = On

Surface Placement		
Rotate	90.000	
Urepeat	1.000	
Vrepeat	2.000	
Uoffset	0.000	
Voffset	0.000	
Mirror	ON	OFF
Stagger	ON	OFF
Chord Length	ON	OFF

Texture surface placement

Tip: *Notice the small triangular slider on the texture window; moving it up will give you a better preview resolution of the texture.*

- Direct render the cylinder.

    The rendered image now shows a smooth material indication.

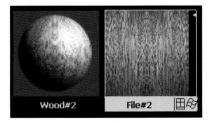

Preview resolution

Smooth wood color

2 Color bump

The same way you reloaded a saved texture for the wire mesh, you can also use the same wood texture for both color and bump. By saving the color file and reloading it into bump, you will ensure that both textures line up, as they will have the same amount of U and V repeat.

- Save the color wood texture as you did before.

- On the shader, click on **Map** next to **Bump**.

- Reload the saved color texture into bump.

- Set the **Intensity Amult** of the bump map to **0.1**.

  If the intensity is too high, the bump will look pixelated.

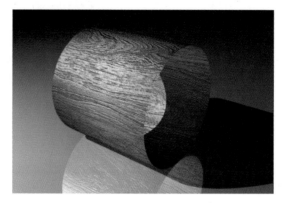

Finished wood with bump map

Carbon Fiber

Although using images to simulate specific materials usually creates the best results, some of the default textures can be modified to achieve similar effects.

- Create a new blinn shader and assign it to the cylinder.

- Click on the **Map** button next to **Color**.

- In the texture window that pops up, select **Grid**.

- Change the grid parameters as follows:

  Line Color = Black

  Fill Color = 15% Grey

  U/Vwidth = 0.4

  Blurmult = 1

  Bluroffset = 0.6

  Rotate = 45

  U/Vrepeat = 40

Chapter Five

- Direct render the scene to evalute the result.

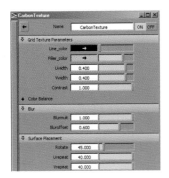

Carbon texture parameters

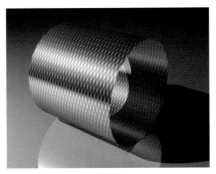

Finished carbon fiber texture

LEDs

Incandescence takes out the dark areas of a shader, making it appear as if it is lit from within. It is a very useful parameter for LED lights and LCD screens.

For a successful LED light, create a blinn shader and assign it to a sphere that resides inside a small cavity.

- On the shader, change the color to a bright red.

- Make the **Incandescence** a medium dark red color.

Too much incandescence will flatten the shape of the sphere.

- Add some **Translucence** and **Glow**.

In the following example, the red dot of the Alias logo was replaced with a sphere that has incandescence and glow on it. Notice how the main lighting has been dimmed a bit to enhance the effect.

LED parameters

Glowing LED light

Lesson 10

LCDs

To create the effect of a LCD screen you will have to map the screen image on both color and incandescence.

- Map the screen texture onto the color of the shader that is assigned to the screen.

  If you render the image now, you will see the graphics on the screen, but they will look flat, like paper.

- On the shader, **Map** the same file onto **Incandescence** as well.

  This will make the screen very bright.

- Adjust the **RGBmult** of the file mapped onto incandescence to be about **75% grey**.

  This will enhance the luminescence of the screen graphics, without looking overexposed.

- Add some **Glow** to the shader to enhance the effect.

LCD screen

Keep non-glowed image

Because the effects of the glow can be unpredictable sometimes, you can also choose to keep the non-glowed image in addition to the one with glow.

In the Render Globals, under Miscellaneous, turn on the option to keep the non-glowed image.

If you render now you will get *two* images, one with and one without glow.

Keep non-glowed image

Chrome

Chrome works best if you have geometry that can reflect into your surfaces. One of the most efficient methods of simulating chrome is by having large incandescent planes above the geometry that will reflect.

- Create a large primitive plane and move it above the cylinder.

- Assign a new blinn shader to the plane and map **Bulge** onto its **Incandescence**.

- On the bulge map, set the **U/V repeat** both to **1**.

    This will make the plane appear to be lit up like a light box.

- Create a new blinn shader and assign it to the cylinder.

- Set the following parameters:

    Specular = white

    Reflectivity = 1

    Color = black

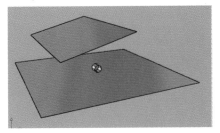

Reflective plane

If you now raytrace, you should get a high contrast image of the cylinder reflecting both the ground and the plane above.

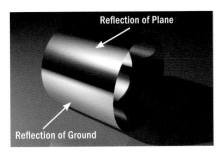

Chrome settings

Chrome cylinder

Stitching

To create stitching effects, you can extrude a circle along a curve on surface that has been projected onto a surface.

- Assign a **Lambert** shader on the extrude.

- Map a Ramp onto its Transparency.

- Set the **Ramp Type** to **V Ramp**. Set the **Vrepeat** to the number of stitches that you want. Turn on **Chord Length**.

The stitching effect is very powerful for accurate design representation and can be equally important as partlines to define shape.

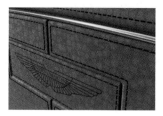

Ramp parameters

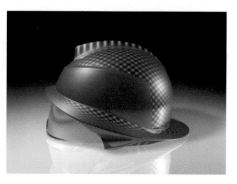

Stitching shader

Projections

Any texture that you map onto any parameter in the shader follows the surface geometry. In some cases, however, you may want to have direct control on how the texture applies onto the surface, or you may want to have a texture go across multiple surfaces, making the geometry look as if it is one solid object. The helmet surfaces have the same carbon fiber shader assigned to them. Notice how it applies itself onto each surface individually and how it stretches uncontrollably. In this case, you want to use a projection to apply the texture onto all surfaces equally.

Regular texture

Note: *Use one of your completed models for this exercise.*

- Save the **Grid** texture into your texture directory as before.

- Assign a new blinn shader to the geometry.

- Click on the **Map** button next to **Color** and chose **Projection** under **Solid** in the pop-up window.

A projection is just another way of applying a texture onto a surface, but it still needs a texture attached to it to work.

- In the Projection window, chose **Map** for **Source Texture**.

Choose projection

Map source texture

- Click on **Browse** and then choose the **Grid** texture that you just saved.

  This will, by default, project the texture onto your surfaces from above.

- Click on the icon in the lower right-hand corner of the projection.

  This will make the projection box visible in the Perspective view. The arrow on the box indicates the upper left-hand corner.

Choose browse

Toggle projection box

- Move, scale and rotate the projection box until it is slightly larger than the geometry.

Lesson 10

Lesson 10
Layering shaders

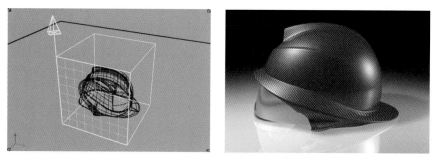

Position projection box   *Projected grid texture*

Take a look at the rendered image. The color map is now being projected on the entire object, making it look like one material. With a spherical shape, such as this helmet, using a projection type other than **Planar** could create additional realism to the texture.

- Open up the projection options. Change the projection from **Planar** to **Spherical**.

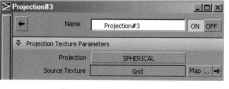

Change projection type

Spherical projection

Tip: *Try to experiment with the different projection types to see their effects on the surfaces.*

Layering shaders

To layer one shader on top of another, you will need a base shader and one with transparency, such as the wire mesh.

- Assign a new blue blinn shader to the cylinder.

Select the wire mesh shader
and layer it onto the first one
by going to:

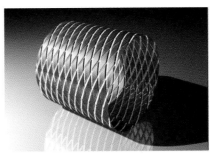

- **Multi-Lister → Shading →
  Layer Shaders.**

  *This will place the wiremesh on
  top of the base shader. If you
  render now, you will see that
  the base shader is showing
  through the transparent areas
  of the wire mesh.*

Layered shader

Tip: *To reverse the process, simply assign a different shader to the geometry.*

Another method is to create a **Layered Shader**.

- Go to **Multi-Lister → Edit → New Layered Shader.**

- Assign the new shader to the cylinder.

- Double-click on the shader to open the options.

  *In the layered shader window that will open, you can now easily add
  or remove shaders and also change the order in which they will apply
  to the surface.*

- Select the blue shader in the **Multi-Lister** and then click on **Add** in the **Layered
  Shader** window.

- Repeat this process with the wire mesh.

  Notice that the icon of the shader also shows the layered effect.

In the layered shader window, you can add multiple shaders to the hierarchy. To
change the order in which they apply, select a name with the **MMB** and move it
up or down.

Tip: *When working with layered shaders, keep in mind that the layers need to
have some transparency, otherwise you will not be able to see through them.*

Lesson 10

Clear coat

To create a shiny clear coat paint effect, you can layer a clear phong shader on top of a base blinn shader.

- Assign a blue blinn shader to the cylinder.

- Create a new phong shader that is transparent with white specular and a very high shininess.

- Layer that new phong shader over the blinn and render it out.

  In the rendering, notice that the base blinn shader is giving the cylinder nice surface definition, while the layered phong shader adds a sharp highlight, which makes the material appear very shiny.

Layered shader parameters   *Layered clear coat*

Logo

In order to project a logo onto a surface, you will have to use a layered shader. Start out by creating two versions of the logo, one that is entirely black and white for the transparency map, and one that has the full range of colors for the color map. Make sure they are identical, on a square canvas and save both in your pix directory as an **RGB tiff**, **jpeg** or **Alias pix** file.

Transparency map   *Color map*

Chapter Five

1 Transparency

- Assign the carbon fiber shader to your geometry.

This will be the base color.

- Layer a new grey blinn shader on top of that.

This will later become the logo.

- Make that second shader completely transparent.

- On that layered shader, click on **Map** next to **Transparency** and choose **Projection**.

Map projection onto transparency

- On the map button in the projection, choose **File**.

Map file onto projection

- Add the black and white map into the file texture.

- Turn the **Wrap** to **Off** in the projection.

This will keep the texture from repeating outside of the projection box.

Map the black and white file   *Turn the wrap off*

Lesson 10

2 Color

Repeat the same process for the color map.

- On the layered shader, click on **Map** next to **Color**.

- In the texture window, choose **Projection**.

- In the projection window, click on **Map** and then **File**.

- In the file window, choose the *color* map that you saved earlier.

- Turn the **Wrap** to **Off** in the projection.

This projects the color texture in the same area as the transparency map.

3 Positioning

To have the geometry receive the logo, you will have to position the two projection boxes first.

- Click on the projection box icon of *both* projections to make them visible.

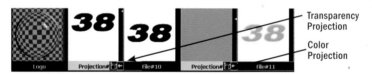

Toggle projections

- In the Perspective view, select *both* projection boxes.

They are on top of each other, so they will appear as one.

- Position the projections so that they intersect with the geometry.

The arrow indicates the upper left-hand corner of the projection.

- Once both projections are in the correct position, direct render the scene to evaluate the effect.

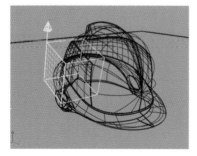

Position projection boxes

Projected logo

LEARNING DESIGN WITH ALIAS® STUDIOTOOLS™

4 Emboss

You can also add an embossed logo effect if you reload the same projection used for the transparency into the **Bump** of the layered shader.

- Save the projection that is mapped onto transparency.

- Click on **Map** next to **Bump**.

- In the texture window, select **Browse**.

- Reload the projection that you have just saved.

- Invert *both* the projection and the file mapped onto bump.

Projected bump map

Conclusion

Aside from the materials and textures covered, you learned how to use transparency, specular, color, bump and incandescence. In addition, you are now able to use layered shaders and projected logos to enhance your rendered images.

In the next lesson, you will understand light parameters and learn light effects.

Lesson 11

Light effects

This lesson will introduce you to the different light types and some of the enhancing effects that you can achieve with them.

In this lesson you will learn to:

- Understand light parameters;

- Create light types;

- Use fog;

- Create lens flare;

- Use light maps.

Light Parameters

Light type ———— Makes the lightsource emit glow, good for light bulbs.

Turns the light on/off. ———— Makes the lightsource emit a halo, good for lens effects.

Turns the shadows on/off. ————

Turns the shadows on/off when in Toggle Shade mode. ———— Makes the lightsource emit fog, good for atmospheric effects.

Makes the lightsource emit lens flare.

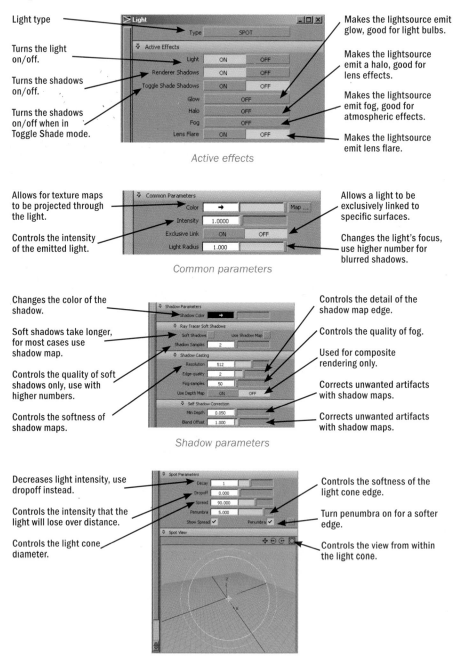

Active effects

Allows for texture maps to be projected through the light. ———— Allows a light to be exclusively linked to specific surfaces.

Controls the intensity of the emitted light. ———— Changes the light's focus, use higher number for blurred shadows.

Common parameters

Changes the color of the shadow. ———— Controls the detail of the shadow map edge.

Soft shadows take longer, for most cases use shadow map. ———— Controls the quality of fog.

Controls the quality of soft shadows only, use with higher numbers. ———— Used for composite rendering only.

Corrects unwanted artifacts with shadow maps.

Controls the softness of shadow maps. ———— Corrects unwanted artifacts with shadow maps.

Shadow parameters

Decreases light intensity, use dropoff instead. ———— Controls the softness of the light cone edge.

Controls the intensity that the light will lose over distance. ———— Turn penumbra on for a softer edge.

Controls the light cone diameter. ———— Controls the view from within the light cone.

Spot parameters

Light types

1   Spot light

The spot light is probably the best light type for just about any light situation, especially when lighting cars and products. It shines out of a cone and is limited to one direction. In the following image, notice how the light intensity gradually decreases in the distance.

Spot light

2   Point light

The point light is much like a light bulb or candle; it has one source and shines in all directions. Notice how much more of the background is illuminated. The point light is great for illuminating spaces or larger surface areas.

Point light

3   Directional light

The directional light is supposed to mimic sunlight. The rays fall parallel in one direction and illuminate everything evenly. The directional light is good for fast renderings, however, it tends to flatten the image. Notice how the ground plane is illuminated evenly and how the image has less depth.

Directional light

Lesson 11

4 Ambient light

The ambient light is a combination of point and directional lights. It has one source that shines in all directions just like the point, and it also flattens like the directional. The ambient light can be used as a substitute for reflective light, however, it often appears flat.

Ambient light

5 Linear light

The linear light is much like a row of point lights. It has one linear source and shines in all directions. It has a very nice soft light, but tends to increase rendering times noticeably in raytracer mode. The linear light can be used to imitate the effects of neon light tubes.

Linear light

6 Area light

The area light is much like a rectangular surface that emits light. It also has a very nice soft light, but also increases rendering time *very* noticeably in raytracer. The area light can be used to imitate the effects of light boxes.

Area light

7 Volume light

The volume light resides inside a shape; by default, it is in a sphere. The shape can be resized, rotated and placed so that the light does not affect any other areas of the image. The volume light can be used for lighting environments or to create specialized effects.

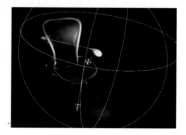

Volume light

Fog

Using fog effects can greatly add atmosphere to a rendered scene. In the following image, **Linear Fog** with an intensity of **0.5** was used with raytracer.

- In the shadow parameters, turn on **Use Shadow Map**.

  Notice that using shadow maps will actually give you a more realistic effect in having the fog display the shadowed areas.

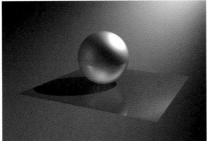

Linear fog

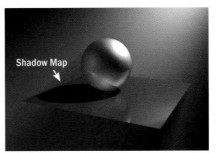

Shadow Map

Fog with shadow map

You can also change the color of the fog or add a texture to it.

- Click on the **Map** button next to the color of the fog parameters.

- Choose a **Solid Fractal** to simulate a smoky environment.

When you look into the cone of the light, you can also use **Radial Noise** to create streaks in the fog, simulating light rays that cast through leaves or water.

Solid fractal fog

Radial fog

Lesson 11

The following example shows a combination of **Linear Fog**, **Radial Noise**, **Halo** and **Lens Flare** to create the light effects.

Combined light effects

Light maps

You can also map textures onto the color of the light, which will turn it into a projector. In the following example, a logo was used on the color of the light to create a branded effect.

Light with logo as color

Conclusion

In this lesson you learned about the different light types and parameters available to enhance your renderings. Together with the previous lessons that covered camera and shader effects, you will now be able to create much more realistic and dynamic images.

Assignment 5

Using these texturing techniques, take one of your previous assignments and texture it to provide a photorealistic and tactile feel. Try to add as much life into your scene as possible and render it full screen.

STUDENT GALLERY > Next page

BELLA CHU

"Bella decided to make a cemetary and achieved an almost surreal environment. I like how the candles by the gravestones illuminate the textures, while the moon casts a cool light onto the scene. Notice how she put my name on one of the graves... I thought that was very clever."

BRIAN WEN

On Brian's image, it took me a while to see that it is actually done in StudioTools because it is so photoreal. I love the cropped composition with one of the note sheets on the keys. The wood texture and logo also worked out very convincingly."

CHAD DEJONG

"Chad cut up a coffe cup, scanned it and mapped the textures onto revolved shapes. This image also made me look twice because it is so photoreal."

ROBERT THOMPSON

"This image has a lot of different texturing techniques to create a clean, luxurious feel. Robert added the girl in the bathrobe after the image was done rendering. I like how it adds a human touch and life to the overall effect."

Chapter Six >

Transportation design

Lesson 12   Automotive Surfaces

In this lesson you will learn how to create tangent surfaces typical to automotive design. You will use the Square and Project Tangent Tools to produce seamless transitions and learn how to utilize temporary construction surfaces for an even flow of the edges. In addition, you will follow simple exercises to build a hood, roof segment, wheel well and surface detail.

In this lesson you will learn how to:

- Use square and construction surfaces;

- Create tangent surfaces;

- Build a car hood, a roof segment, a wheel well, a surface detail, an air intake and a pocket;

- Construct three-sided and two-sided surfaces.

Square

The **Square Tool** is similar to the **Rail Tool**, but *always* requires four curves to build. It can serve as an alternative surface tool if rail is not producing the desired results.

1 Curves

- Begin by sketching a simple curve in the *side* view window.

  This will place it along the X-axis.

- Sketch out two more curves in the *top* view, each snapped to the first curve, and each perpendicular to the X-axis.

  *Use the **RMB** to place the second CVs.*

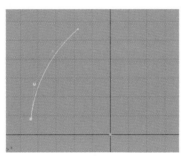
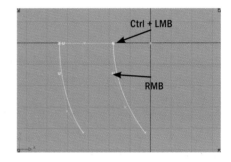

Curve in side view   *Add two curves in top view*

Note: *If the second CVs are not perpendicular, you will get a seam later on.*

Add a fourth curve that connects the previous two, mapping out a rectangular shape as shown.

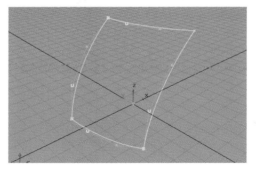

Four curves

2 Square

Now create a simple square surface by going to:

- **Palette** → **Surfaces** → **Boundary Surfaces** → **Square** → ◻.

- In the options, set the first curve's **Continuity** to **Implied Tangent**, and click on the first curve on the centerline.

- Continue clicking on the remaining three curves and the **Square** will be created.

Select first curve

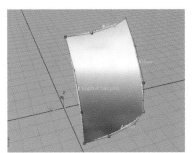

Square surface

3 Check symmetry

- Assign the four curves used onto a new layer named *Curves* and make that layer invisible.

  This is important so that you do not accidentally select the curves again later on.

- Assign the **Square** to a new layer and turn on **Symmetry** to make sure that there is no seam down the center.

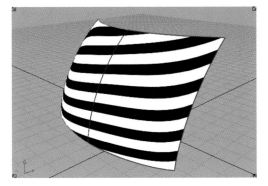

Seamless symmetry

Lesson 12

Tangent square

1 Curves

For the next curves, use a **Curve Degree** of **5** by going to:

- **Palette** → **Curves** → **New Curves** → **New Curves By CVs** → ☐.

- In the options, select a **Curve Degree** of **5**.

  This will place out a new curve that is using six CVs, which allows for greater control over the resulting surface.

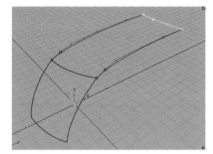

Curve degree of 5

- Create two more curves that will continue forming the first **Square**.

  *Make sure to snap the first CVs on the edge of the surface by holding **Ctr + Alt**.*

- Create a third curve, connecting the previous two.

  *Switch the **Curve Degree** back to **3** and place it in the top view so that you can make the second CV perpendicular as before.*

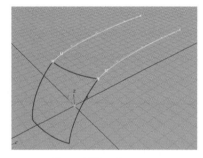

Two additional curves   *Third curve*

2 Project tangent

Use the **Project Tangent Tool** on both curves touching the surface to create tangency.

- **Palette** → **Curve Edit** → **Project Tangent** → ☐.

  Leave the option window open, because you will adjust the settings in the next step.

- Click on the edge of the curve and then on the edge of the surface.

  You will see the project tangent parameters as shown below.

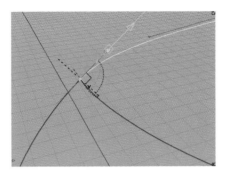

Project tangent

- With the Project Tangent Tool options still open, change the **Xform Control** to **Curvature**.

  Notice how the third CV will adjust its position to follow the curvature of the surface.

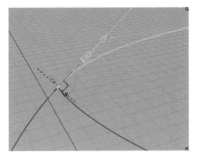

Project tangent options   *Project tangent with curvature*

- Use Project Tangent on the second curve as well.

Tip: *You may have to adjust the remaining CVs to ensure an even flow in the curves.*

---

3 Tangent square

- Use the Square Tool again to create a second surface.
- In the square options, set the second curve's **Continuity** to **Tangent**.

When selecting the curves, make sure that the surface edge is the second curve.

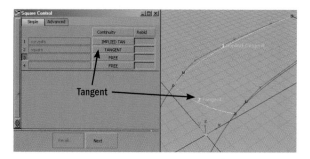

Tangent on surface edge

- Continue to select the remaining two curves.

- Assign curves and surfaces to their respective layers, and turn on symmetry to view the result.

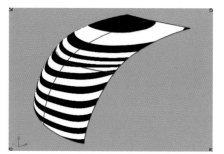

Tangent surfaces

Hood

The last exercise has left little control over the side edges of the surfaces. In this next step you will gain greater control over the flow of the geometry from all angles.

1   Temporary rail

- Delete the previous square surfaces, but keep the curves.

- In the *top* view, sketch out an additional curve as shown.

  It will serve as the primary rail curve for a temporary surface.

- In the *back* view, sketch another curve that touches the first.

  This one will serve as the generation curve.

- Create a simple rail surface as shown.

Chapter Six

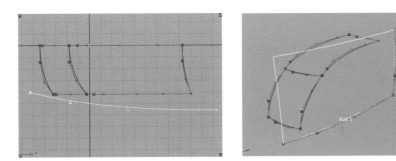

Primary rail curve	Temporary rail surface

2 Project curves

Select the rail in the side view and go to:

- **Palette** → **Surface Edit** → **Create Curve on Surface** → **Project** → □.

- In the options, make sure that the output is set to **Curves**, and that **Match Original** and **Create History** are set to **Off**.

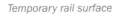

- Click on **Go** and select the two inner curves to be projected onto the surface.

  Make sure that you are in the side view when you project the curves onto the surface.

Project options

The resulting new curves now have much greater control over their flow.

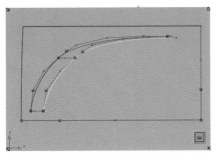

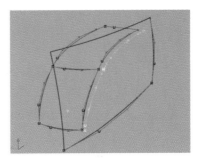

Project inner curves	Projected curves

3 Organize file

- Assign the rail surface and the two curves that created it to a new layer and turn its visibility off.

- Assign the two original curves that you have used for projection to that layer.

  What you are left with are five of the original curves and two projected ones. Notice that there is a gap between the new and old curves.

- Adjust the CVs of the cross-section curves to ensure that they touch the end CVs of the projected curves.

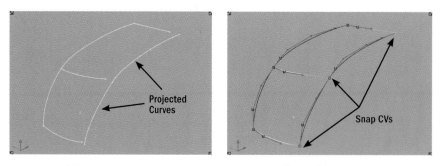

Old and new curves   *Snap CVs to curves*

4 Square

- Repeat the two **Square** surfaces as before, using **Implied Tangent** for the centerline, and **Tangent** for the shared edge of the two surfaces.

  Notice the even flow on the surface edges as a result of using the temporary surface.

This technique could be used to model the hood of a car, either with square or rail surfaces.

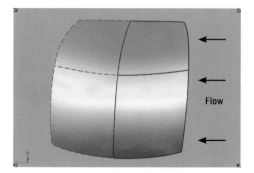

New square surfaces

Roof segment

The same technique of projecting curves onto surfaces can be used in conjunction with the Rail Tool.

- In the *side* view, sketch out a total of three curves as shown below.

  The third curve is a horizontal connection to close off the inner one.

- Sketch out another curve in the *top* view.

  This will become a primary rail curve.

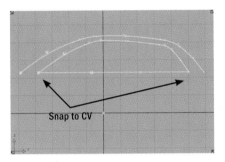

Three curves

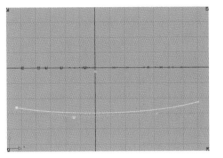

New curve in the top view

- Create a generation curve as shown here, and make a rail surface.

- In the *side* view, project the inner curves onto the surface to create two curves on surface.

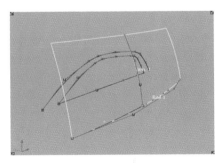

Rail surface

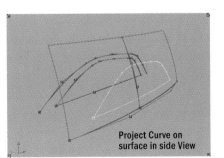

Two projected curves on surface

- Trim the rail surface.

- Assign all unnecessary curves to a separate layer and make it invisible.

Lesson 12

Lesson 12
Roof segment

- In the *top* view, create two generation curves that are snapped to the center curve and the surface.

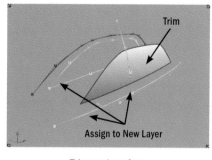

Trimmed surface

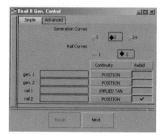

Add generation curves

- Create a rail surface.

- In the options, set the primary rail to **Implied Tangent**, and **Rebuild** the second rail.

  Because the second rail is a trimmed edge, the rebuild option will create a smoother surface.

Rail options

- Click on the two generations curves, and then select the centerline as the primary rail and the trimmed edge as the secondary.

- Assign the used curves onto the invisible layer.

- Use the **Round Tool** to create a fillet.

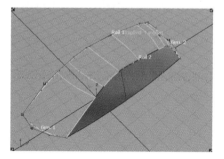

Finished rail surface

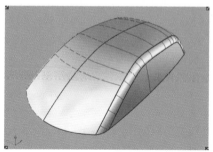

Finished roof segment

Wheel well

Create a subtle rail surface and a plane that is slightly offset.

- In the side view, create three concentric circles as shown below.

  The two smaller circles must fit onto the width of the plane.

- **Rotate** all three circles clockwise until the **U** is *below* the surfaces.

  Otherwise, you will have problems constructing the surfaces later on.

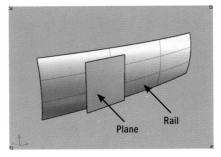

Rail and plane

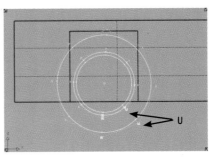

Three circles

- In the *side* view, project the two smaller circles onto the plane, and the larger one onto the rail surface.

- Trim away both surfaces, leaving only a thin rim from the plane.

- Delete the circles.

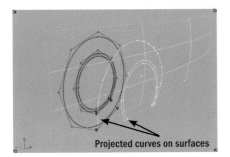

Three projected curves on surfaces

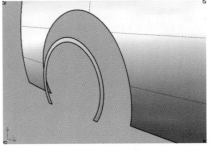

Trimmed surfaces

- Create a curve using **Edit Points** with a **Curve Degree** of **5**.

- Snap the first and last CVs to the surfaces.

Lesson 12

- Add another curve for the other side.

  This will give you two generation curves that can be railed along the trimmed edges.

- Go to the Rail Tool and create a surface.

  *Make sure to **Rebuild** at least one of the rails.*

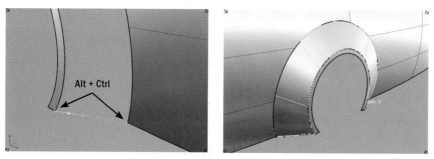

Add curve with edit points   Straight rail surface

Rebuilding the rails will give you an industrial design look. To create a smooth transition between the surfaces, delete the rail surface first and go back to the Project Tangent Tool.

- **Palette → Curve Edit → Project Tangent → ☐.**

  *The **Xform Control** should still be set to **Curvature**.*

- Click on the edge of the curve, and then on the edge of the surface.

  This will make the curve tangent to the surface as before.

- Repeat this step three more times until both curves have **Curvature** to both surfaces.

- Go back to the Rail Tool, but this time choose **Tangent** for both rails.

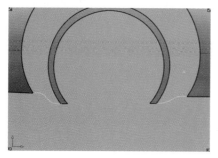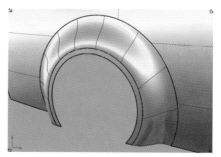

Curves with project tangent   Smooth rail surface

Chapter Six

Character line

To create a character line on a surface, you will have to trim away a section of it first. Use the rail surface from the previous exercise.

- Sketch out two connecting curves in the *side* view.

  Make sure both curves extend over the edges of the rail surface.

- Still in the *side* view, project the two curves onto the surface and trim as shown.

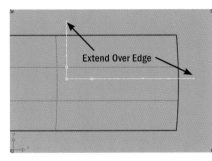

Two curves for trimming

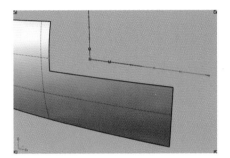

Trimmed rail surface

- Create two curves with a curve degree of 5 that connect to the trimmed section.

  On the shorter curve, place the CVs so that the curve will form a step, as shown.

- Use the Project Tangent Tool on the two curves as before.

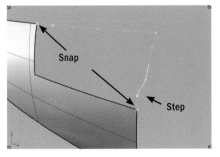

Two character curves

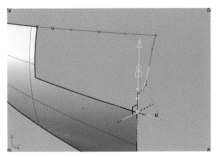

Project tangent

- Create a rail surface with the **Continuity** of **Generation 1** and **Rail 1** set to **Tangent**.

Lesson 12
Air intake

*You will also have to use the **Rebuild** option on those edges to get a
cleaner result.*

If you turn on diagnostic shading, the new section should appear to blend in
seamlessly with the main surface as shown.

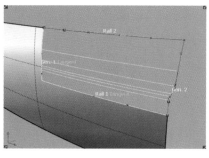

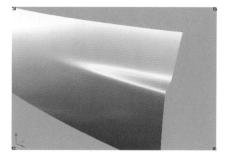

Rail with tangency   *Seamless character line*

Air intake

The same technique can be used to create an air intake, however, there are
a few extra steps involved.

In the *side* view, project a Curve on Surface as shown below.

- Create two curves that are snapped to the Curve on Surface and bend
  slightly inwards.

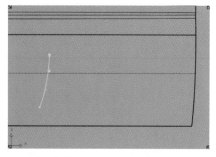

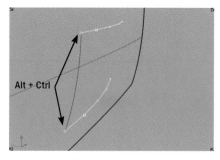

Project curve on surface   *Two rail curves*

- Create a rail surface with **1 Generation** and **2 Rail** curves.

- Set the generation curve to **Tangent** and **Rebuild**.

  This will create the air intake surface and make it tangent to the main body.

- Delete the **Curve on Surface**.

- Assign the two rail curves on a new layer and make it invisible.

- Detach the original curve used to project as shown.

This will give you three segments that you will need to project onto the surface again.

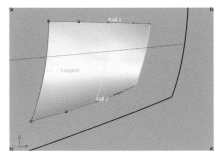

Air intake surface

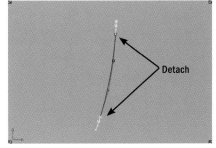

Detach curve

- In the *side* view, sketch out another curve that will be used to trim out the air intake.

Make sure to snap the first and last CVs onto the other curve segments.

- Project this curve onto the surface together with the three segments.

This will give you a total of four curves on surfaces.

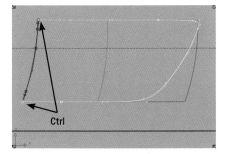

Air intake curve

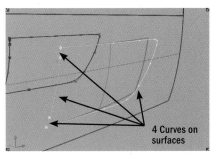

Projected Curves on surfaces

- Trim the air intake out.

- Create another curve in the side view that is snapped to the curve segments and slightly smaller than the air intake.

You will use this curve to trim out the intake surface.

Lesson 12

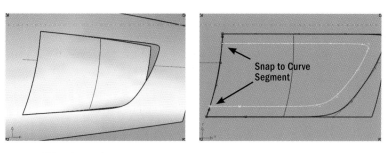

Trim the surface   Intake curve

- Project that curve onto the intake surface and trim it.
- Rail the surface with **Tangency** and **Rebuild On**.

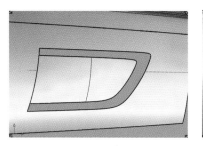

Trimmed intake   Finished rail

- Add detail by projecting curves and trimming.

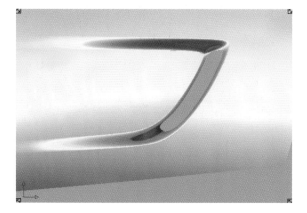

Finished air intake

Three-sided surface

Each and every surface in StudioTools has four edges, without exception. However, you will run into situations in which you have to create the appearance of a surface with only three sides. In the following exercises you will learn a few techniques to build corners.

- Begin by bringing out a primitive cube with a scale of **10**.

- Select the three rear surfaces as a **Component** and **Delete** them.

- Use the **Round Tool** with a radius of **1** on all three edges.

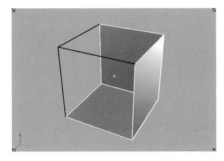
Delete three sides

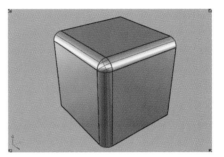
Rounded edges

- Select the corner surface as a **Component** and **Delete** it.

  This will give you the scenario of having to create a three-sided surface, such as the front corner of a car.

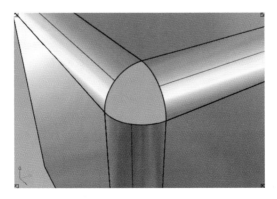
Three-sided scenario

Lesson 12

Lesson 12
Three-sided surface

1 Rail

- Go to the Rail Tool.

- In the options, select **2 Generation** and **1 Rail** curve and set their continuity to **Tangent**.

- Click on the three edges to create a surface.

  Notice that you will receive a surface that pinches together in one of the corners. Although the reflection looks somewhat decent, it does not really qualify for large surface details. With anything more complex than this cube, the pinch would create a noticeable distortion in the surface.

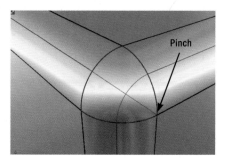

Rail surface

2 N-sided

- Delete the previous rail surface.

- Go to **Palette** → **Surfaces** → **Boundary Surfaces** → **N-sided** → ❐.

- In the options, set the **Continuity** to **Tangent**.

- Click on the three edges to create a surface.

  If you turn on the CVs on the N-sided surface, notice that it is actually a trimmed surface. N-sided can be used between 3, 4, 5 or more curves, but does have its limitations in maintaining seamless transitions.

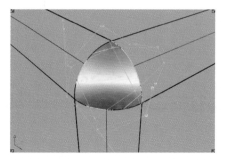

N-sided surface

3   Curve networks

- Delete the previous N-sided surface.

- Go to **Palette** → **Surfaces** → **Curve Networks...**

- In the window that pops up, right-click on **CrvNet Tools** and select **New Network**.

- Click on the three edges and **Go** to create surfaces.

  Notice that the New Network Tool actually creates three separate square surfaces, which is a great way to construct a corner.

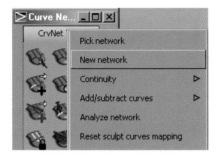
New curve network

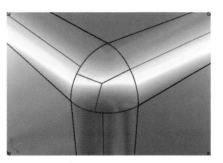
Curve network surfaces

4   Ball corner

- Delete the previous curve network surfaces.

- Go to **Palette** → **Surfaces** → **Ball Corner** → ❐.

  Leave the option window open.

- Click on the three edges and **Go**.

  Notice that you are being asked to select a fourth surface to create a corner.

- Click on the right face of the cube.

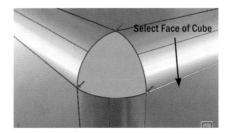
Select fourth surface

- Click on **Go**.

  Notice that you will actually get a four-sided surface that wraps around the face of the cube that you have selected as the fourth surface.

Ball corner surface

- In the options window, adjust the **Start/End Length Ratio** to **0.1**.

  You can also set the **Continuity** to **Curvature**.

  The surface will update automatically.

  The ball corner surface is the most elegant solution from the previous examples because it has the most control and direction.

Ball corner control   *Finished ball corner*

Two-sided surface

Occasionally, you will run into a situation that requires a two-sided surface, typically a rounded crown or similar. The following is just an example of how to construct a four-sided surface out of two edges.

- In the *top* view, create a 180 degree circle and two curves as shown below.

- Create two more curves with **Edit Points** as shown.

  *Use **Alt** + **Ctrl** to snap the edit points to the curve.*

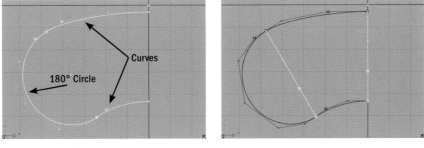

Three curves   *Curves with edit points*

- Move the middle CVs of the two new curves up in the Z-axis as shown.

- Create a rail or square surface as shown.

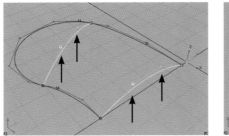
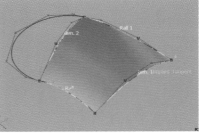

Move CVs   *Rail surface*

- Detach the rail surface twice so that you will get a thin strip in the middle.

- Use the **Extend Tool** to create a small tangent surface.

- In the options, uncheck **Merge**.

  This will create a separate surface.

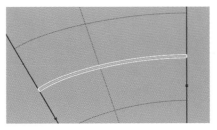
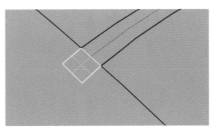

Detach rail   *Extend surface*

- In the *top* view, create a small circular curve as shown.

- Project it onto the **extend** so that you can trim it out.

- Trim the extended surface.

- Create a tangent rail surface.

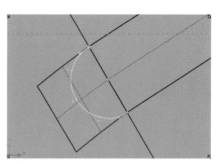

Project curve

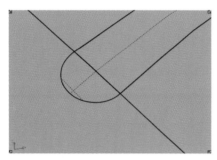

Trimmed extend

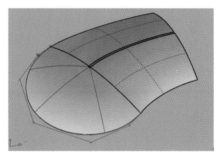

Tangent rail surface

One-sided surface

A one-sided surface type is typically a pocket. Usually, you can create a sphere or similar shape to intersect with the surface, but in some cases you may need to achieve more precise results.

1 Rail surface

- Create a closed circular curve as shown.

  This curve will serve as a visual guide only.

- Assign that curve to a new layer and set its state to **Reference**.

  This will turn it brown.

- Create another four curves that follow the reference closely.

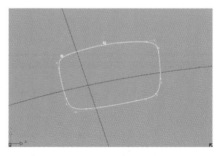

Pocket curve

Chapter Six

- Project these curves onto the surface in the *top* view.

  They will be used to create a rail surface.

- Create another two curves as a visual aid and assign them on the reference layer.

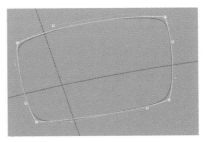

Four curves

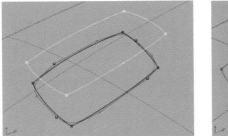

Projected Curve on Surface

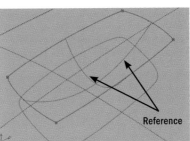

Reference curves

- Use the four curves on surfaces to create a rail surface.

- In the options, turn on **Explicit Control** and set the **Curve Degree** to **5**.

  The resulting rail surface will be modified into a pocket in the next step.

Explicit Control

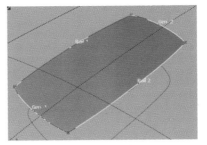

Flat rail surface

2   Construction plane

A construction plane allows you to temporarily change the orientation of the entire grid, and is extremely useful when you have to model at an angle.

- Go to **Palette** → **Construction** → **Plane**.

- Use **Alt + Ctrl** to snap the plane onto the reference curve.

Lesson 12

- Rotate the plane using the handles until it follows the reference curves.

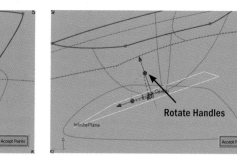

Place construction plane

Rotate construction plane

- Click on **Accept Points**.

- Click on **Set Construction Plane**.

Notice that now the entire grid is using the new construction plane.

- Select the interior CVs of the rail surface in the *top* view.

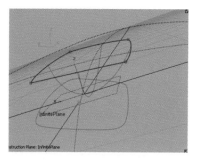

Set construction plane

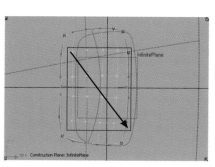

Select CVs

- Snap them to the grid in the *side* view.

- Go to **Palette → Construction → Toggle Construction Plane**.

This will set the views back to their original state.

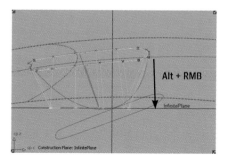

Snap CVs to the grid

Tip: *You can also choose and delete the construction plane like a regular object.*

3 Pocket

- Select the four Curves on surfaces and delete them.

- Intersect the pocket with the main surface to create a new Curve on Surface.

- Select the four corner CVs of the pocket surface in the *top* view.

- Move the CVs slightly up in the Z-axis until the Curve on Surface matches your reference underneath.

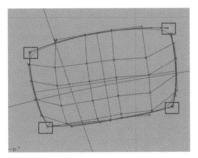
Select corner CVs

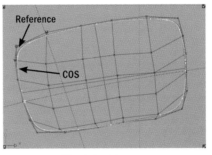
Match both curves

- Trim both surfaces back to evaluate the result.

  At this stage you could also add a small fillet around the edge.

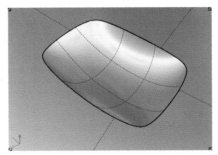
Finished one-sided surface

Conclusion

In this lesson you learned some of the basic techniques for constructing various automotive surface types that you will likely encounter when building a real vehicle. You are now ready to use the Square and Rail Tools together with projected curves and temporary geometry to model the car in the next lesson.

Lesson 13   Car

In this lesson you will use many of the previously learned techniques such as rail, project and square to build a full car. Note that automotive companies build their vehicles without the use of symmetry to maintain better control over the reflections across the centerline. Also note that this lesson is geared towards using the previously covered tools; depending on your design there may be other ways of constructing the surfaces.

In this lesson you will learn how to:

- Build the main car body;

- Create a shoulder;

- Build the roof segment;

- Build the wheel wells;

- Adjust the flow of intersections;

- Add finishing detail.

Main body

1   Top surface

- Sketch out two sets of curves in the *side* view.

  The outer ones are the silhouette and the inner ones will be used as character lines.

- Add two sets of concentric circles.

  These will be used later to create the wheel wells.

- Create another two curves and use them to create a rail surface.

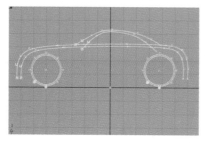
Curves in the side view

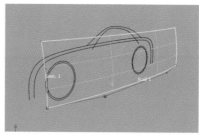
Temporary rail surface

- In the side view, project the inner curve onto the surface.

- In the options, choose **Curves** and **Match Original**.

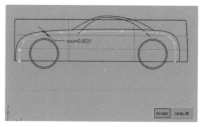
Project curve onto surface

- Assign the rail surface to a new layer and make it invisible.

- Add two generation curves connecting the profile curves.

  Make sure to place the second CVs perpendicularly. In the example shown, three additional generation curves were placed in-between to help maintain continuity of the surface.

- Create a rail surface with **Rail 1** set to **Implied Tangent**.

  Turn on symmetry to make sure there is now a seam down the centerline.

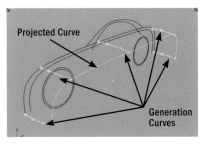

Generation curves

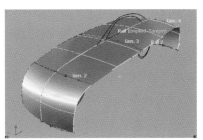

Top rail surface

Tip: *You could also use the Square Tool for this step.*

2   Shoulder and side

- Create another curve in the side view for the shoulder line.

- Create another rail surface for the side of the car body.

- In the *side* view, project the shoulder line onto the surface to create a Curve on Surface.

- Trim the side body as shown.

- Add additional generation curves between the two surfaces.

  In this case, five generation curves are used.

- Rail between the two surfaces.

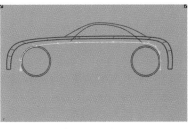

Shoulder line

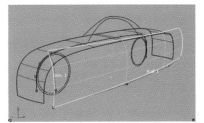

Side body surface

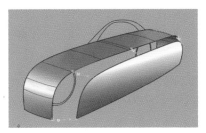

Trimmed side body

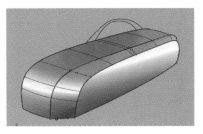

Finished car body

Roof segment

1 Side window

- Create a curve that is touching the shoulder line.

- Rail that curve along the shoulder line.

- In the *side* view, project the inner window curve onto the surface to create a Curve on Surface.

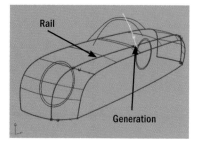

Window curve

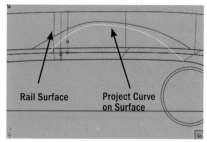

Project window Curve on Surface

2 Roof

- Trim the side window and create two generation curves.

   In this case, an additional generation curve was used in-between.

- Create a rail surface with implied tangency for the centerline.

- Fillet the surface edges.

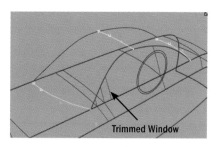

Roof curves

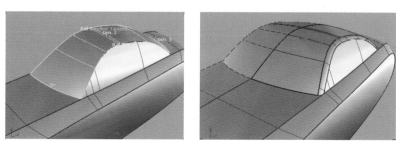

Roof surface

Finished roof segment

Chapter Six

Wheel well

1   Surfaces

- Create two surfaces for the wheel wells, as shown below.

  In this case, primitive planes were used and the CVs adjusted to create some subtle curvature.

- In the side view, project the circles onto the surfaces to create Curves on Surfaces.

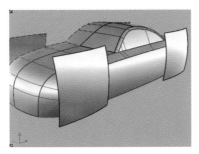

Primitive planes

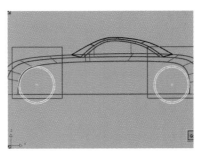

Project circles

- Trim the surfaces back as shown.

- Create another temporary rail surface and project two larger circles onto it.

  The resulting Curves on surfaces will serve as the second rails.

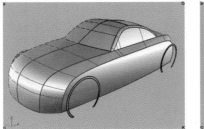

Trimmed accents

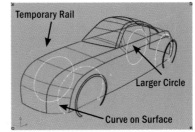

Temporary rail

- Add three generation curves as shown.

- Create a rail surface.

- Repeat the process for the rear wheel.

Lesson 13

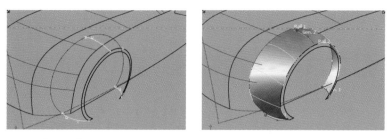

Generation curves   Wheel well

2   Adjustment

Notice how the previous technique left an irregular intersection between the two surfaces.

- To achieve a better flow you can Detach the rail surface and delete the lower segment.

- Intersect the remaining surface with the shoulder of the car.

  This will give you a lead Curve on Surface.

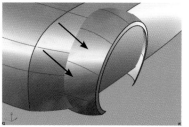
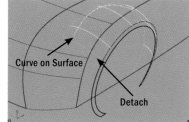

Irregular intersection   *Detach surface and intersect*

- Create a new curve in the *back* view and project it onto the shoulder.

- Create a new rail surface with the generation set to **Tangent**.

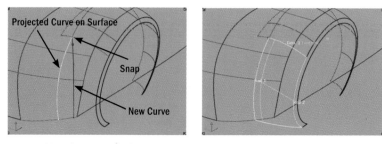

New Curve on Surface   *New rail*

Bottom surfaces

- At this stage you can add additional small curves to create bottom rail surfaces around the car body.

- Trim the surfaces back and evaluate the result.

- Add detail and the wheels from the previous assignment to finish the car.

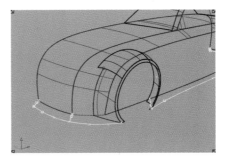

Rail curves

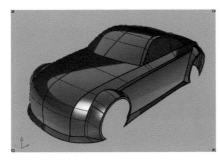

Finished car body

Finished car

Conclusion

In this lesson, you learned how to apply all modeling techniques explored thus far into building a full car. Simple surfaces were constructed to quickly build the body and roof, while detailing helped to make the vehicle more realistic.

In Lesson 14, you will learn how to animate your geometry within StudioTools.

Assignment 6

Design and model a full car and environment, reusing the wheels from Assignment 3. Add as much detail to the vehicle as possible to achieve a photorealistic effect and render the image full screen.

STUDENT GALLERY > Next page

Lesson 13

KEVIN KANG

"Kevin made beautiful use of the modeling tools covered, all put together with adequate details and strong lighting effects. Notice the use of reflections to define the form of the car as well as the interior indication. Overall excellent execution."

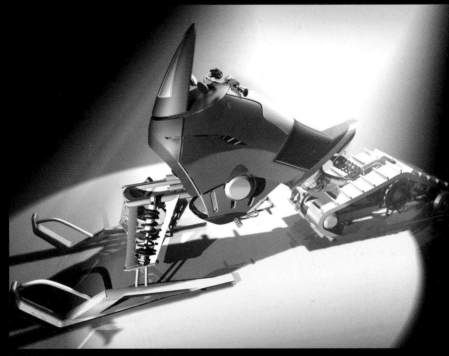

GREG STOERMER

"Greg went for a snowmobile and managed to put an extraordinary level of detail together with a well executed form. The outcome is a unique, yet realistic design approach, which makes the object very tangible."

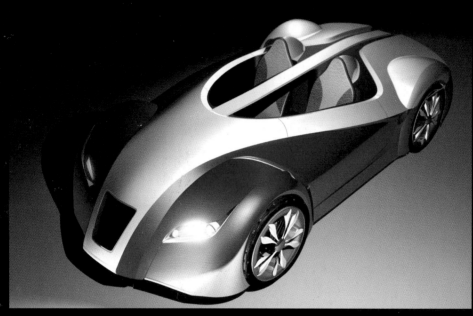

SO YON CHRISTINE PARK

"I like Christine's playful use of shape and proportion in her car. Notice how even the set-up is less dramatic, the form still reads strong and distinct due to the clean modeling. Well done!"

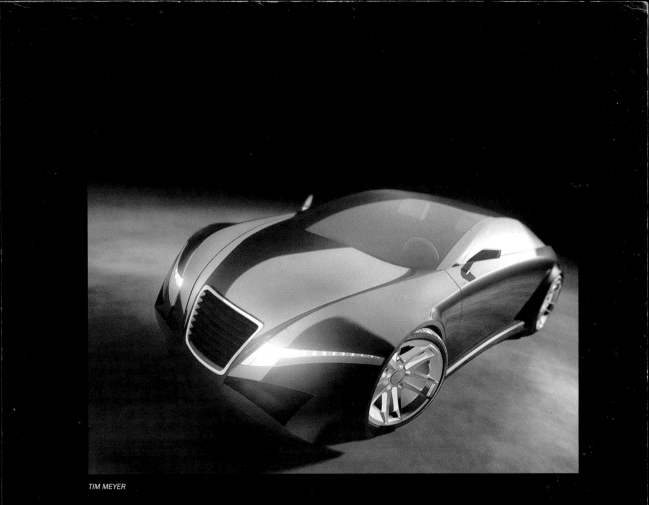

TIM MEYER

"What a powerful image Tim created! Notice the flawless surfaces as defined by the white reflection from above. Notice how the tilted composition adds to the dynamic of the whole image. There is not much I could have done better to this rendering."

Chapter Seven >

Animation

Lesson 14   Animation basics

In this lesson you will learn some of the animation capabilities within StudioTools. Animating your geometry can serve a variety of purposes, such as evaluating the design and to show concepts or functions for client presentations. You will begin by setting some keyframes on simple geometry to familiarize yourself with the principle of animation. Following are small exercises that will teach you specialized scenarios and tools, as well as how to animate the shaders lights and cameras. Finally, you will render out your own animation to evaluate the results.

In this lesson you will learn how to:

- Use the animation controls, the action window, parameter control, anim sweep and clusters;

- Set keyframes and edit keyframes;

- Set motion paths;

- Set expressions;

- Animate a car;

- Animate the camera;

- Animate shader and light parameters;

- Render animations;

- View animations.

Bouncing ball

1 Animation controls

To make the animation controls visible, go to:

- **Studio** → **Animation** → **Show** → **Toggle Time Slider** ...

This will add another window above the modeling windows.

Tip: *All animation tools used in this lesson are located under* **Animation.**

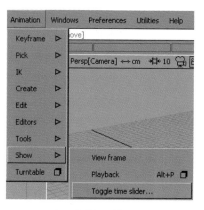

Toggle Time Slider

The **Time Slider** consists of multiple parts and controls used to control the animation.

- On the left side, switch **Min/Max** to **Start/End** by clicking on it.

- Set the **Frame Range** to **1** and **90**.

Left side of Time Slider

- Set the **frames per second** (**FPS**) to **30**.

Right side of Time Slider

2   Setting keyframes

- In the *side* view, place a sphere to the left of the **Z-axis**.

- **Scale** the sphere to **2** and place it one unit above the **X-axis**.

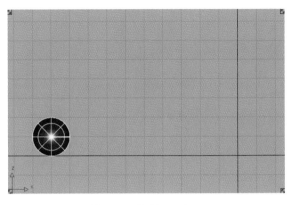

Place a primitive sphere

With the sphere still active, go to:

- **Studio** → **Animation** → **Keyframe** → **Set Keyframe** → ☐.

- In the options, set the following parameters:

> **Parameters = Local;**
>
> **Hierarchy = None;**
>
> **Frame = Prompt;**
>
> **In/Out Tangent = Linear;**

- Click on **Go**.

- In the promptline, enter the number **1** and press **Enter**.

  This will lock-down the sphere's current position at frame 1.

- Using the **MMB**, move the sphere to the right on the **X-axis**.

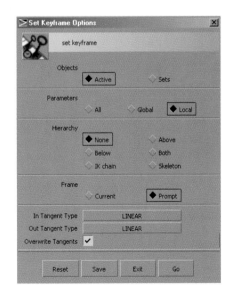

Keyframe options

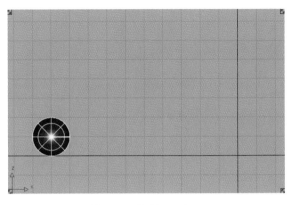

Lesson 14

- Go back to **Set Keyframe** and click on **Go**.

- This time enter **90** in the promptline and press **Enter**.

If you now click the **Play** button in the **Time Slider**, the sphere will move across the X-axis in 90 frames, or three seconds.

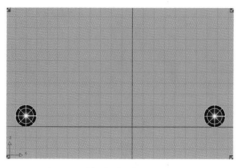

Moving sphere

3   Add rotation

- Move the **Time Slider** to frame **90**.

- Select the sphere and go to **Rotate**. In the promptline, enter:

    0 1000

This will rotate the sphere roughly three times in the Y-axis.

- Press **Enter**.

Proceed to overwrite the current frame with the new rotation.

- Go back to **Set Keyframe** and enter **90** in the promptline again.

When you press Enter, you will get a warning message asking if you want to overwrite 9 keyframes. Click Yes and playback the animation. The sphere is now rolling across the X-axis.

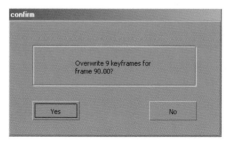

Overwrite keyframes

Note: *The reason for the nine keyframes is because you set them on the sphere's* **Rotation,** **Translation** *and* **Scale** *in* **X,** **Y** *and* **Z,** *which is a total of nine channels.*

4 Action window

Open the **Action Window** to see the nine channels by going to:

- **Studio** → **Animation** → **Editors** → **Action Window...**

  You will see the nine animation curves, consisting of a green one that goes off the chart (Y Rotate), a red one (X Translate) and a few static ones that are linear.

Tip: *You can navigate in the action window just like you would in the Orthographic views by using* **Alt + Shift.**

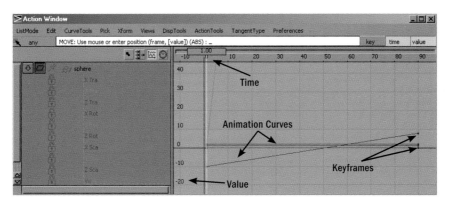

Action window

The action window displays the animation in terms of *value* (vertical axis) and by *time* (horizontal axis). Since some of the animation curves are static, meaning they do not change over time, you will have to delete them to keep the animation clean.

- Go to **Studio** → **Delete** → **Animation** → **Delete Static Actions.**

  You will be asked to confirm – click yes.

Lesson 14

This will delete the unused animation channels from the sphere. Notice how some of the horizontal animation curves have been deleted in the action window.

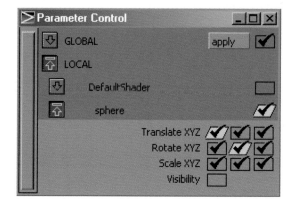

Deleted animation curves

Tip: You can also delete the entire animation by choosing **Delete Channels**.

5 Bounce

To avoid setting keyframes on all nine channels simultaneously, open up the **Parameter Control** window to isolate the **Translate Z** channel.

- Go to **Studio** → **Animation** → **Editors** → **Param Control...**

Notice how all channels are selected, but only two have animation on them as indicated by their slanted boxes and lighter color.

Parameter control

- Uncheck everything
  except for **Translate Z**.

  *If you now set keyframes,
  only the Z Translation
  channel will be affected.*

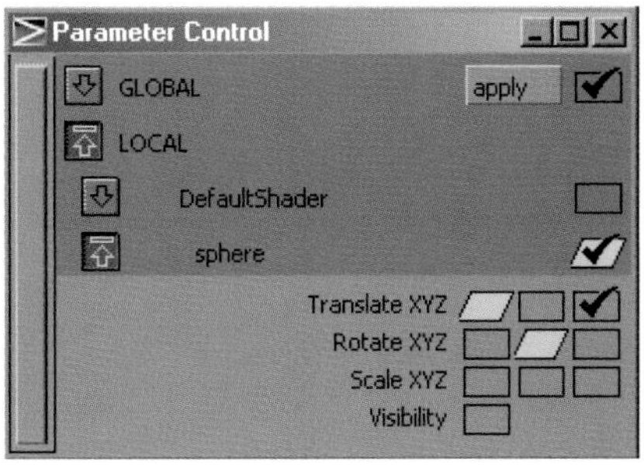

Isolate Z Translation

- Go to **Set Keyframes**.

  *Type the following frames in the promptline for the sphere's
  down position:*

  1 30 60 90

- Press **Enter**.

  *In the action window you will see a straight animation curve for
  Z Translate with multiple keyframes on it. This indicates that the
  sphere will be in its down position at those frames.*

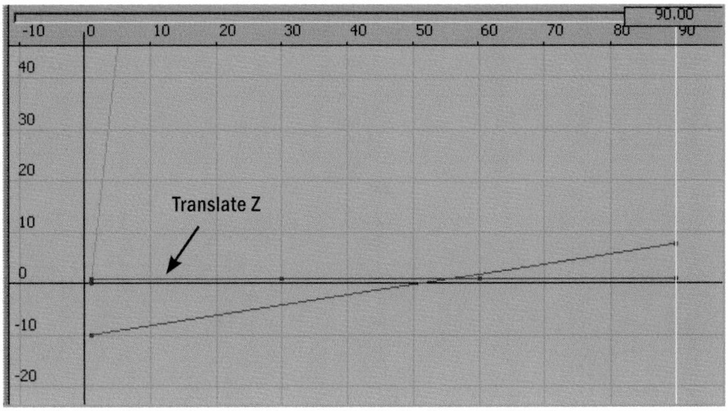

Animation curve for Translate Z

- Move the sphere up a few units above the Z-axis.

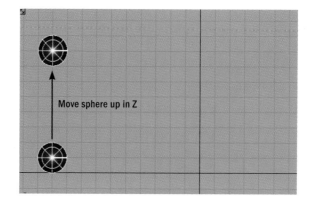

New sphere position

- Go to **Set Keyframe**.

- Type in the following frames in the promptline for the sphere's *up* position:

   15 45 75

- Press **Enter**

   Notice in the action window that the animation curve for **Z Translate** *is now showing a zig-zag pattern.*

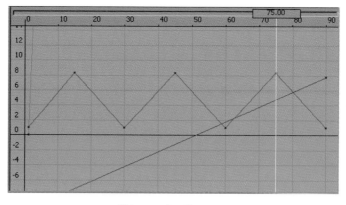

Zig-zag animation curve

If you now play the animation, the sphere bounces statically. To fix this, you will have to select the top keyframes in the action window and change their tangency type.

Tip: *The action window has its own marking menu.*

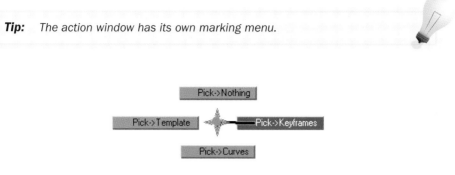

Pick->Nothing

Pick->Template   Pick->Keyframes

Pick->Curves

Action window marking menu

- In the action window, select *only* the three top keyframes of the Z Translate animation curve
- Set their **Tangency Type** to **Slow In**.
- And then to **Slow Out**.

Set tangency type to slow in/out

This will slow the sphere down when it is reaching its peak, making the animation more realistic.

Lesson 14

Motion Path

To animate an object following a curve, you can use the **Set Motion Tool**. Create a sphere at the origin and a curve in the *top* view.

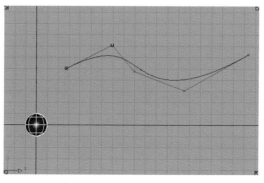

Sphere and curve in top view

With the sphere selected, go to

- **Studio → Animation → Set Motion → ❒.**

    Turn the **Bank Off**;

    Set the **End Frame** to **90**.

You can adjust the start and end frames for a longer animation. The bank options allow the object to tilt inward and outward while following the curve.

Set motion options

- Click on **Go**.

The sphere will turn pink, and you will be asked to select the curve.

- Click on the curve.

The sphere will jump to the first CV. Playback the animation to see the result.

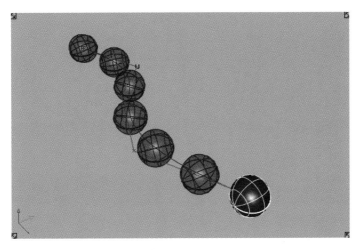

Set motion

Set motion is often used to create realistic movement of vehicles, but you can also set the camera to follow a path, or to use it in combination with **Anim Sweep**.

Anim sweep

The **Anim Sweep Tool** allows you to create surfaces out of animated curves or shapes.

1 Creating animation

Following is an example of how to create a spring out of an animated circle:

- In the *side* view, create a circle to the right of the **Z-axis**.

- Set its pivot to the origin.

Lesson 14

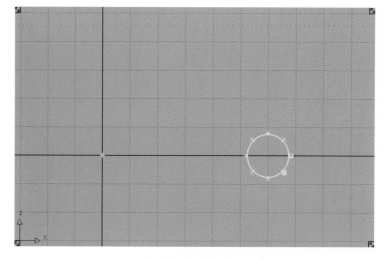

Circle in the side view

- In the **Parameter Control** of the circle, uncheck everything except for **Translate** and **Rotate Z**.

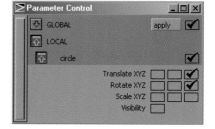

Parameter control

- Set a **keyframe** at **Frame 1**.

- Move the circle up along the Z-axis.

- Rotate it by 1800 degrees around Z.

- Set a keyframe at **Frame 90**.

If you playback the animation, the circle will rotate around Z while moving upwards, producing a spiral shape.

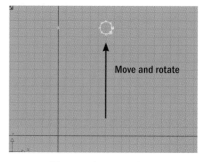

Move and rotate circle

2 Creating anim sweep

To create a surface out of the animation, select the circle first
and then go to:

- **Palette** → **Surfaces** → **Swept Surfaces** → **Anim Sweep** → ❑.

- In the options, set the **Sweep** to **Connect Snapshots**, and the
  By Frame to **4**.

  *Setting the by frame option to a lower number will give you better
  precision but higher geometry.*

- Click **Go**.

  The Anim Sweep Tool will create a surface out of the animation, as shown.

Anim sweep options   *Anim sweep surface*

Lesson 14

Lesson 14
Expressions

Expressions

An expression allows an object to move, scale or rotate based on another objects' animation, thus simplifying cause and effect actions.

- Create two cylinders in the *side* view.

- **Scale** the first one to a size **2**, the other to a **scale** of **4**.

- Rename the small gear *G1*, the larger one *G2* in the **Information Window**.

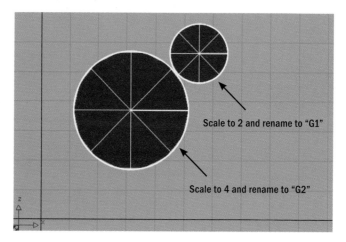

Two gears

You will now write an expression into the action window that will make *G2* the affected gear.

- With the larger *G2* selected, open up the action window.

- Switch to the expression view by clicking the clock icon.

- Type the following expression next to **Y Rotate**:

  G1:RY/ (-2)

- Press **Enter**.

The expression says to read from *G1*: in its rotation in Y (RY) and to divide (/) that value by half (-2). The negative is necessary so that *G2* will rotate in the opposite direction of *G1*.

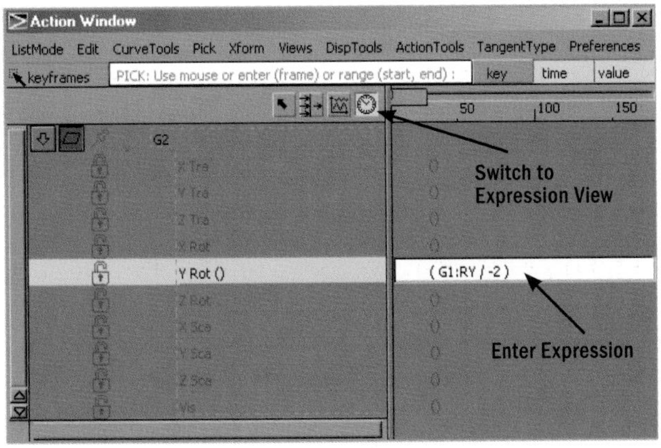

G2 expression

To make the expression update automatically, go to:

- **Studio** → **Preferences** → **Performance Options** ...

- Check **During Transform** under **Expression updates**.

  This will rotate G2 automatically whenever you are rotating G1.

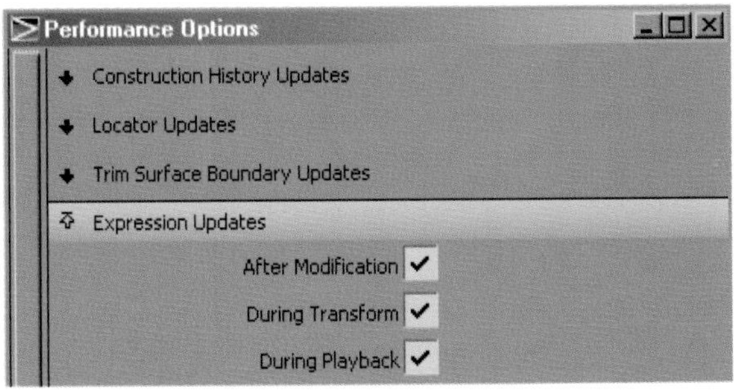

Performance options

Add a third gear by duplicating one of the previous ones.

- Make it a **Scale** of **8** and rotate it so that it is perpendicular to the other two.

- Rename that gear to *G3*.

- Go to **Palette** → **Transform** → **Zero Transforms**.

  This will reset the object's rotation, scale and transform information.

Lesson 14

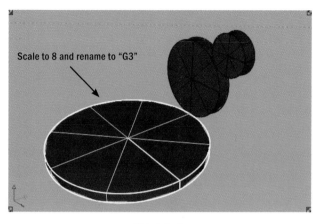

Third gear

- With *G3* selected, type the following expression next to **Z Rotate**:

    G1:RY/ (-4)

- Press **Enter**.

    Notice that both gears are affected by G1, and that they are being affected on different axes.

G3 expression

Try to set a few keyframes on the first gear's (*G1*) **Y** rotation to see the full effect of the expressions.

Car animation

Using the expression techniques, you can easily produce a car animation, where the wheels rotate based on the vehicle's translation.

- Create two cylinders as wheels.

- Name them *W1* and *W2*.

- For the chassis, create a cube and name it *Body*.

- Group all three elements together and name that node *Car*.

Note: *The following numbers will only work if your grid spacing is set to 1 centimeter.*

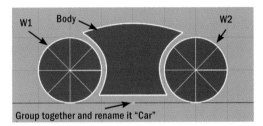

Primitive car

- With *W1* selected, type the following expression next to **Y Rotate**:

    Car:TX* 45

This will rotate the wheel by 45 degrees around Y for every unit of translation of the car in X.

W1 expression

Lesson 14

For the rear wheel, you could write the same expression. However, try to have it read from the front wheel instead.

- With the *W2* selected, write the following next to **Y Rotate**:

  W1:RY

  This will make W2 read from W1.

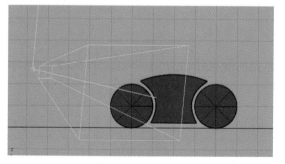

W2 expression

If you now move the car, the wheels will rotate accordingly. Try to set a few keyframes on the car to see the behavior of the wheels.

Animating the camera

1   Freeform

Make the camera visible by going to:

- **Studio → Display Toggles → Object Toggles → Camera**
- Select the camera.

Toggle the camera

- Go to **Studio** → **Animation** → **Keyframe** → **Set Keyframe** → ❐.

- Set the **Hierarchy** options to **Below**.

- Choose **In-Out** for the **Tangent Types**.

  This will make the camera motion appear more natural when it starts and stops moving. Setting the hierarchy options to below is necessary because the camera consists of three grouped parts

Camera keyframe options

- Click on **Go** and enter a keyframe at **1**.

- Move and rotate the camera in the Perspective view and set another keyframe.

  *To view the animation curves, open the **Action Window**. Notice that the curves are static for the top node. To view the actual animated curves, click on the pull-down arrow on the left of persp. This will show the lower nodes of the camera.*

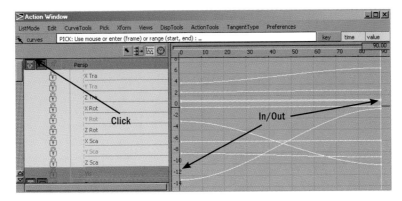

Camera animation curves

Lesson 14

2 Rotation

To create an additional camera, go to:

- **Palette → View → New Camera.**

This will create a second camera, giving you the option to create a different camera animation such as a rotation. To look through the new camera:

- Click on the camera icon on top of the Perspective window.

- Choose **Camera#2.**

To add a rotational animation:

- Select the camera in the *top* view.

- Set a **keyframe** at frame **1**.

- **Palette → Transform → Rotate.**

Switch between cameras

- Enter a rotation of **0 0 90** in the promptline.

  This will rotate the camera around its pivot point.

- Set another keyframe at frame **90**.

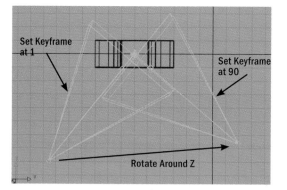

Keyframe camera rotation

This technique also allows you to create full 360 turntable animations, which are great for evaluating a design.

3 Specify output camera

Before rendering, make sure that you specify which of the two cameras will actually output the images. To render using the new **Camera#2**:

- Go to the **Globals**.

- Scroll down to **Image File Output**.

- Select the new camera as shown.

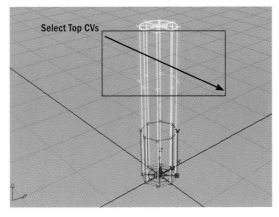

Select output camera

Clusters

To animate CVs for flexible objects, you have to first turn them into a **Cluster**. A cluster is a group of CVs that co-exists independently from the regular geometry and has its own node in the Object Lister.

1 Create a cluster

- Create a cylinder with two caps.

- Select only the top CVs of the geometry as shown.

Select CVs

- Go to **Studio** → **Animation** → **Create** → **Cluster**.

  Notice that the selected CVs turn blue to indicate that they are now in a cluster.

Create cluster

Object lister

In the **Object Lister**, notice the new node that is independent from the cylinder. You can select the cluster either here, or by going to:

- **Studio** → **Animation** → **Pick** → **Cluster**.

Also notice that the cluster has its own blue pivot point.

2   Animate cluster

- With the cluster selected, set its pivot about half way up the cylinder.
- Set a keyframe at frame **1**.
- Rotate the cluster 90 degrees in the Y-axis.
- Set another keyframe at frame **90**.

If you now playback the animation, you will see the cylinder bending to the right over 90 frames.

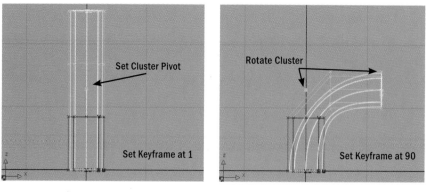

Set cluster pivot

Rotate cluster

Clusters can become complex to work with, as they exist in addition to the regular geometry. However, they are extremely powerful when animating flexible objects such as live hinges, chords and plastics.

Animating shaders and lights

The process for setting keyframes on shader and light parameters is different than for objects because you will use the Time Slider instead of the **Set Keyframe Tool**.

- Set the **Time Slider** to the Frame **10**.

This will become the first keyframe.

Set Time Slider

- Open a shader and using the **LMB** + **Shift-click** on the word **Color**.

It will become indented, showing that it is active.

Select color

- Using the **RMB**, click on the word again and select **Keyframe**.

This will set a keyframe for that RGB value at frame 1. Notice the small slanted animation icon that will appear next to color: it is an indication that keyframes have been set.

Set keyframe

- Move the **Time Slider** to frame **80**.

This will become the next keyframe.

Set Time Slider to 80

Lesson 14

- Change the color **RGB** to **blue**.

- **Right-click** on the word **color** again and **select Keyframe**.

  This will now set a keyframe for that RGB value at the Time Slider location, which is 80.

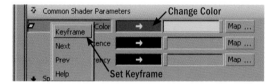

Keyframe new color

You can now see the keyframes in the action window and modify them if necessary.

Color animation curve

Note: *If you now playback the animation, the shader may not update its color in real time. Instead, use hardware shade or render out the animation.*

Using this technique, you can virtually animate any light or shader parameter, which will give you the power to both add life and concept to your animation. Think about animating the transparency of a product to show its components, or animate LEDs to show function.

Rendering animations

Once you have animated a few objects, shader parameters and the camera, you can render the frames out into an animation.

1 Test renderings

Direct render a few different frames of your animation to make sure that the rendering quality is acceptable and that the geometry is well lit.

2 Globals

- In the **Render Globals,** check the **Animation** box.

  Notice that you will get an option to specify the range of frames to be rendered. In most cases, you can leave it at **Time Slider.**

Check animation

- Under **Image File Output,** choose either **Alias** or **Tiff** format for the rendered images.

  If you are planning to view the animation only in **StudioTools,** *choose* **Alias Format.** *If you are planning to take the rendered frames to another software for editing, choose* **Tiff Format.**

- Make the render resolution **720 x 486.**

Note: *A larger resolution will dramatically increase the rendering time.*

Image output

Lesson 14

3 Rendering

- Open the rendering options and choose either raycaster or raytracer as you normally would and click on **Go**.

- In the **Save Image** window that appears, create a new folder and open it.

- Give the animation a new name and click on **Save**.

  This will render all animation frames into the new folder, keeping your pix directory clean and organized.

Save animation

4 Viewing animation

Using **FCheck**, you can load all rendered frames into one window and play them back to preview the animation.

- Go to **Studio** → **Animation** → **Show** → **FCheck** ...

- In the window that appears, go to **File** → **Open Animation** ...

- Open the file that you just rendered.

  *Notice that only the first frame is displayed. If you open the animation it will load all the frames into the **FCheck** window and then play them back.*

Chapter Seven

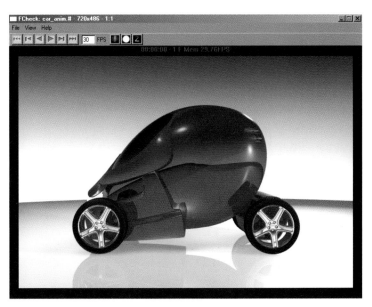

FCheck animation

Conclusion

You have just learned some of the animation capabilities within StudioTools by setting keyframes on geometry, cameras, shaders and lights. Although animations can sometimes take a long time to render, they can be essential to conceptual presentations.

In the next lesson, you will learn about Alias ImageStudio™ software.

Assignment 7

Using one of your previous assignments, create a 20-30 second animation with the tools and techniques covered in this tutorial.

Lesson 14

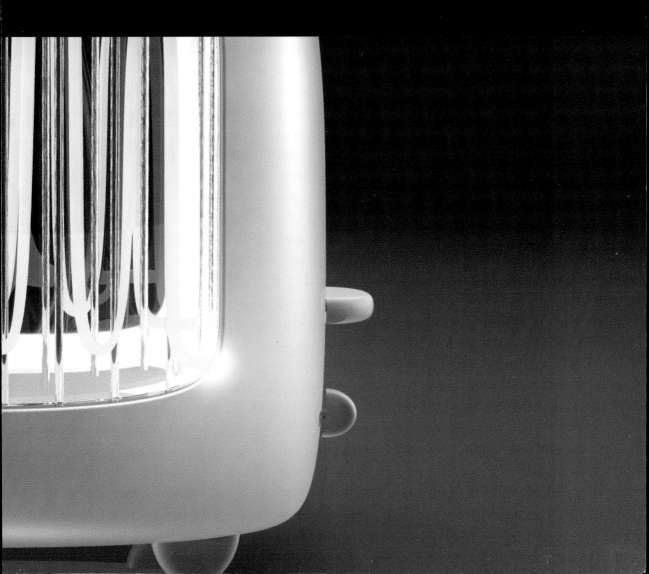

Chapter Eight >

Alias ImageStudio

Import geometry

Begin by importing one of your previous assignments. In Alias StudioTools, prepare the file so that it is clean with no shaders or lights, and with each component saved onto a different layer.

- In **ImageStudio** go to **File → Import Model...**

  This will show the model in a neutral color and environment.

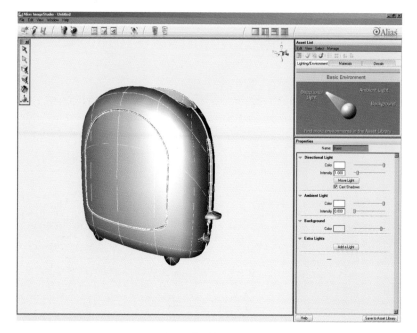

ImageStudio layout

- Switch the layout to a horizontal configuration by clicking the button on the top bar, as shown below.

  Depending on your geometry, you could also choose a vertical format.

Switch layout

- Click on the **Refresh** button under **Render Now** as shown.

  This will instantly render the scene in a default environment.

Alias ImageStudio -
File Edit View Windo

Render Now
Refresh   Final
Adjust Quality...

Render now

Tip: Use Alt + Shift and the RMB to zoom in and out of the rendered image in the top window. You can also navigate the preview window on the bottom the same way that you navigate the Perspective view in StudioTools.

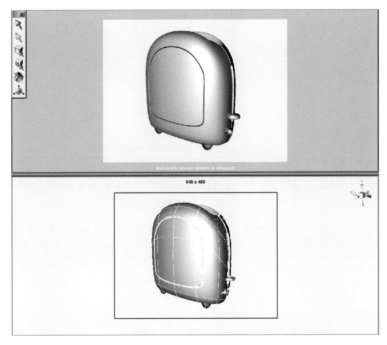

Horizontal layout

Asset List

1   Create materials

- Click on the **Asset Library** button in the **Asset List** on the right panel.

  In the window that opens, you will see a selection of default environments and materials.

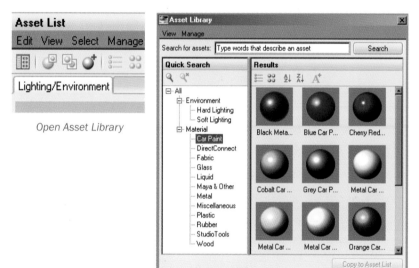

Open Asset Library

Asset Library

- For your model, double-click on any materials that you like.

  *This will automatically load them into your **Asset List** on the right panel.*

Tip: *The **Asset List** is the same as the **Multi-Lister** in StudioTools.*

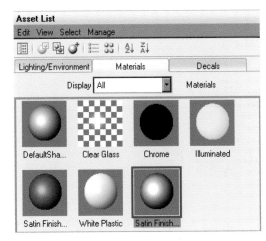

Asset List

2   Assign materials

There are a few different ways of selecting the geometry.

- Open the layer window by going to **Window** → **Layers.**

  If your geometry was saved on different layers, you can select all content by clicking on the arrow icon.

Select layer

- To better see which geometry is selected, switch to **View** → **X-Ray** or **Wireframe.**

  You can also select geometry by using the selection panel.

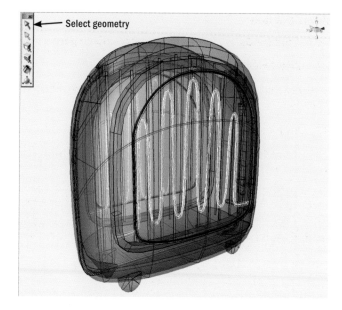

X-ray view

- To assign a material to selected geometry, double-click on it in the **Asset Lister**.

- After assigning all materials, click on the Refresh button to render the scene.

Test render

3 Modify properties

- Hold down **Shift + Ctrl + LMB** to bring up the **marking menu**.

- Click on **Clear Selection**.

  This will make sure that you do not accidentally reassign materials to different surfaces.

- Click on any material to change its properties.

  Notice how the test rendering is updating automatically with each change.

Change properties

Create environments

- Go back to the **Asset Library**.

- Double-click on an environment such as **Skylight**.

  This will automatically load the environment into the Asset Lister. To change the environment, just double-click on any other choice.

- Refresh the test rendering to evaluate the result.

Lesson 15

Lesson 15
Create environments

Revised rendering

- You can set the floor position in the environment properties.

Set floor position

- Adjust other properties, such as the color of the floor or the background, as needed.

  You can also add another light to see its effect.

- Set the final image size as needed.

Final image size

- Click on the **Final** button under **Render Now**.

Create final

This will create a more polished and final image.

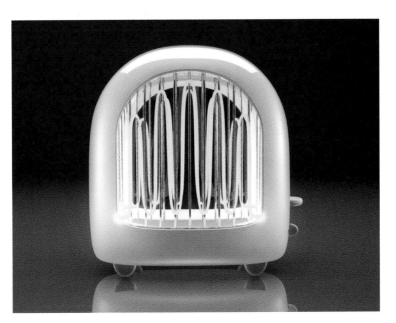

Refined rendering

Conclusion

In this lesson you learned how to use ImageStudio to quickly create photorealistic renderings. The more experience you gain with its intuitive interface, the better you will become at creating and assigning materials and rendering scenes.

In the next lesson you will review some common problems and easy solutions for unexpected problems you may encounter with StudioTools software.

Lesson 15

Chapter Nine >

Troubleshooting

Rendering failed

When you begin using Alias StudioTools, creating something in the wire file that prevents rendering can easily occur. Most commonly, it is a trimmed surface that fails to tessellate. It can also be caused by a shader that has an incompatible texture map assigned to it. In either case, the surface or shader probably needs to be deleted or recreated.

renderer.exe

renderer.exe has encountered a problem and needs to close. We are sorry for the inconvenience.

If you were in the middle of something, the information you were working on might be lost.

Please tell Microsoft about this problem.
We have created an error report that you can send to us. We will treat this report as confidential and anonymous.

To see what data this error report contains, click here.

Send Error Report   Don't Send

Error message

1   Delete all shaders

Start troubleshooting your file by deleting elements until the file renders. *Save your file first* and then begin deleting all shaders.

- Go to **Multi-Lister** → **Delete** → **Shaders**

- Try to render the scene.

  If the file renders, then one of your shaders was causing the problem.

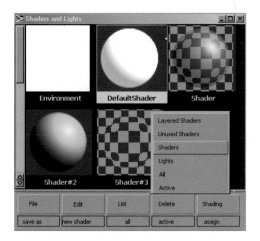

Delete all shaders

- Go back to the *saved* file and delete the shaders one by one until the file renders.

Once the file renders, you will know that the last shader that you deleted was causing the problem.

2 Delete all geometry

If the file did not render in the previous step, then proceed to delete the geometry. If your file has all geometry on separate layers, you can easily select and delete it. Make sure you have saved your file under a new name first.

- Pick all objects on the first layer.

- Delete that geometry.

- Try to render the scene.

  Repeat these steps until the file renders. Once the file renders, you will know that the surface causing the problems was on the last layer that you deleted.

Pick objects

- Go back to the saved file and examine the surfaces on that specific layer one by one.

  Once found, you will have to delete and rebuild that surface.

3 Revert to 9.0 Tessellator

In some cases, especially with IGES file formats or complicated trimmed surfaces, you can use the 9.0 tessellator to render the geometry that failed earlier.

- Open the **Render Globals**.

- Under **Global Quality Parameters**, turn on **Revert To V9.0 Tessellator**.

- Set the **Quality Type** to **Global**.

  *The **Adaptive Minimum** and **Maximum** values allow you to control the tessellation amount for all surfaces.*

      Higher numbers = smoother surfaces

Revert to 9.0 tessellator

4 Copy and paste

In rare cases, there might be geometry that is either invisible or completely trimmed, or there might be another corrupt element in the file that fails to render. Save the file first, then select the entire visible geometry and go to:

- **Studio → Edit → Copy.**

- **Studio → File → New.**

  Click **Yes** *on the window that pops up.*

- **Studio → Edit → Paste.**

  This technique sometimes helps to eliminate certain corrupt and non-visible elements.

Long rendering times

Unusually long rendering times, most often while raytracing, are typically caused by either heavy geometry, lights, or high Render Globals.

1 File cleaning

Clean your file of *anything* that is not needed, but remember to save first.

- **Pick → Curves** (+delete).

- **Pick → curves on surfaces** (+delete).

- **Pick → Template** (+delete).

- Select all geometry and then **Delete → Construction History**.

- Delete any layers that are invisible, such as the curves layer.

- **Studio → Layers → Delete → Unused Layers**.

- **Multi-Lister → Delete → Unused Shaders**.

- And, finally, copy and paste all geometry into a new file and save it with a *new* name.

   You should notice a smaller file size.

2   Shrink to trim

Trimmed surfaces will maintain their entire surface data and thus greatly increase the file size. To fix this, you can shrink the trimmed surfaces.

- Go to **Studio → Utilities → Plug-in Manager…**

- In the window that opens, select the **ShrinkToTrim** plug-in.

   This will automatically load the plug-in.

- Select the entire geometry.

- Go to **Palette → Surface Edit → Trim → + ShrinkToTrim**

- Click **Go**.

   This will shrink all selected trimmed surfaces. If you now save the geometry under a new name, you should notice a smaller file size.

Plug-in manager

3   Lights

- Try not to use more than two-six total lights.

   More lights will increase rendering times noticeably.

- Try to only have one-two main lights casting shadows.

   More shadows will increase the rendering time.

- When raytracing, try *not* to use **Linear** or **Area Lights**.

   They will greatly increase rendering time.

Lesson 16

Tip: *Try to* **Use Shadow Maps** *whenever possible. Although they are not as precise or refined as regular shadows or even soft shadows, they will render much faster.*

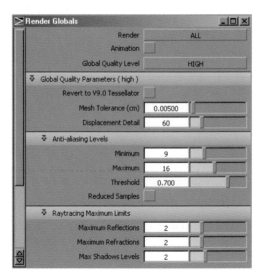

Use shadow map

4 Render Globals

- When rendering, try to use numbers between **9-16** for the **Anti-aliasing**.

  Using higher numbers will increase the rendering time noticeably.

- When raytracing, try to use numbers between **2-4** for the **Raytracing Maximum Limits**.

  Higher numbers will increase the rendering time noticeably.

Suggested Render Globals

Rendering problems

When rendering an image, you may encounter some seemingly strange problems that are usually easy to fix.

1 Texture flipping

If you notice a texture file that previously rendered fine, but all of a sudden either flips upside down or is mirrored, it might be due to a conflict with the **tiff** file used.

- Try to resave the tiff file as either a **jpeg** or **Alias Image File** and re-assign it.

  This will usually solve the problem.

Texture flipping

Tip: *You can use fcheck to load a tiff file and save it as an Alias pix file.*

2 Lights out

If your scene renders black or very dark, you might be working on a larger grid than described in this book.

- Try to scale your entire geometry down so that it fits onto a 40 x 40 cm grid.

Lesson 16

- Make sure your lights are not accidentally assigned to a layer that is invisible.

- Make sure there is no geometry in front of the light that might be blocking it.

> **Tip:** *You can also increase the light intensity to a much larger value, such as 100-200. However, it is easy to overexpose the lighting this way.*

3   Artifacting

If you notice a surface that is displaying some strange patterns when rendered, it is usually an indication that you have two surfaces on top of each other.

- Try to select the duplicate surface and delete it.

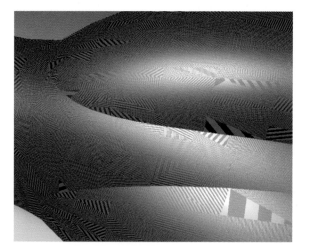

Artifacted surface

Printing

To render an image so that it can be printed at a specific size and quality, you must first calculate its pixel dimensions.

In most cases, your DPI will be between 150-300.

Chapter Nine

- If you want to render an 11 x 17 image that can be printed at 200 DPI, multiply the dimensions by the resolution:

  11in x 200dpi = 2200 (use for the Y resolution)

  17in x 200dpi = 3400 (use for the X resolution)

- Enter the desired numbers in the **Render Globals**.

- Change the **render format** to **tiff**.

Print resolution

Note: *When you now render the file, give the name a **.tif** extension so that other graphic programs can recognize the format.*

Conclusion

In this lesson you learned how to troubleshoot and solve some of the most common problems that you may encounter when first learning StudioTools. If your problem was not addressed in this lesson, be sure to check the StudioTools Help documentation or visit www.alias.com.

Alias
StudioTools™ > GALLERY

DIGITAL CAMERA – DESIGN BY F. BEISERT & F. BUCH

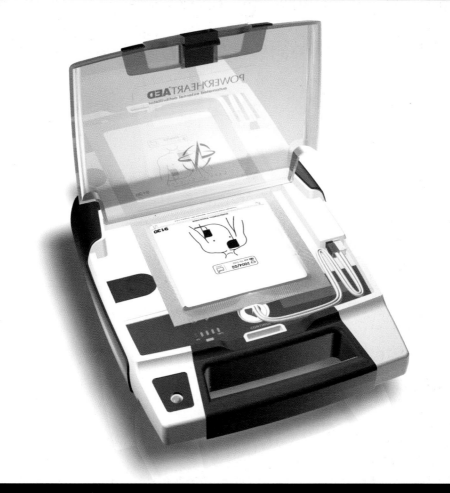

Streichhölzer

MATCHBOX LIGHTER

DIGITAL BOTTLE OPENER – DESIGN BY F. BEISERT & F. BUCH

RECEPTION DESK

CAR – DESIGN BY CALVIN LUK

Alias
StudioTools™ > GALLERY

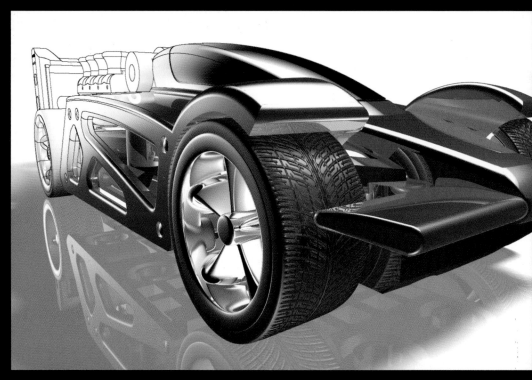

TOY CAR WITH HIDDEN LINE RENDERING EFFECT

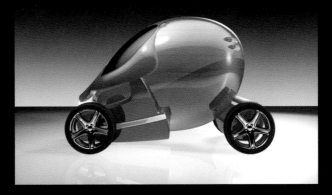

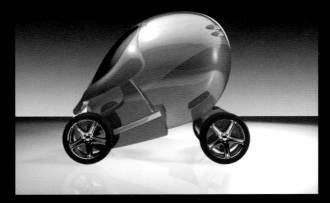

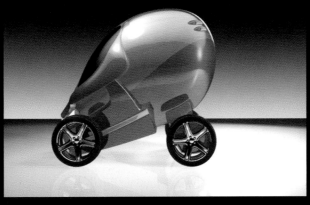

HEAD CAR – DESIGN BY RICHARD LASSALLE

LIGHT CHESS

TRAIN FOR TV COMMERCIAL

BLIMP FOR TV COMMERCIAL

VIDEO GAME VEHICLE

VS SALON – DESIGN BY W. SABA

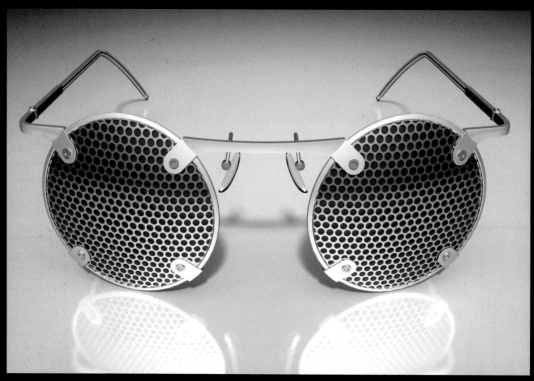

SUNGLASSES

SCREWDRIVER
Product of Sweden

Tripple distilled from premium grains

40%Alc/Vol 80Proof
750ml

PACKAGING DESIGN

Index

AutoCAD
Made Easy as
1 2 3

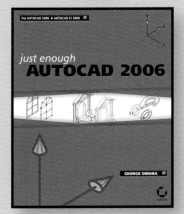

Just Enough AutoCAD 2006
By George Omura
ISBN: 0-7821-4397-0
US $24.99

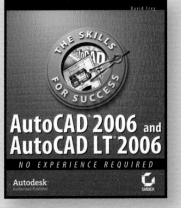

**AutoCAD 2006 and
AutoCAD LT 2006:
No Experience Required**
By David Frey
ISBN: 0-7821-4414-4
US $34.99

**Mastering AutoCAD 2006
and AutoCAD LT 2006**
By George Omura
ISBN: 0-7821-4424-1
US $49.99

The natural way to draw,
the modern way to work.

Alias® SketchBook® Pro, the high quality paint and drawing tool for use with tablet PC's and digitized tablets, has a fast, simple and natural interface that has the tactile feel of drawing with a pencil and paper and all the benefits of a digital format.

The artist friendly, gesture-based user interface of SketchBook Pro is easy enough for the casual user to master, yet has all the features that experts demand. But don't take our word for it. Download a full-featured trial version of SketchBook Pro 2 for Mac® or Windows® at **www.alias.com/sketchbookpro** and try it for yourself.

Alias
SketchBook Pro

DESIGNED FOR
Pen Tablets &
Tablet PCs

Alias | www.alias.com

design

machome

Macworld